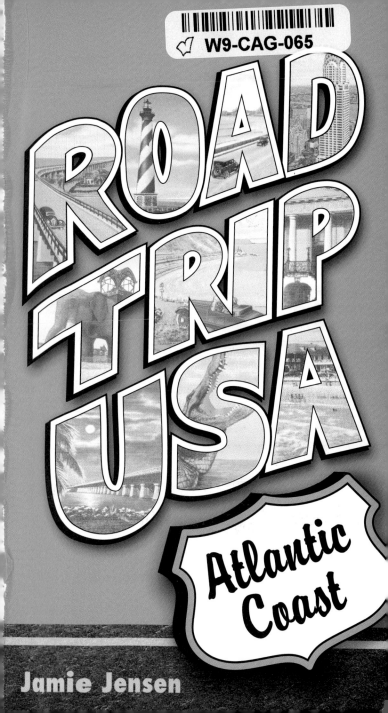

ROAD TRIP USA

Atlantic Coast

Jamie Jensen

Contents

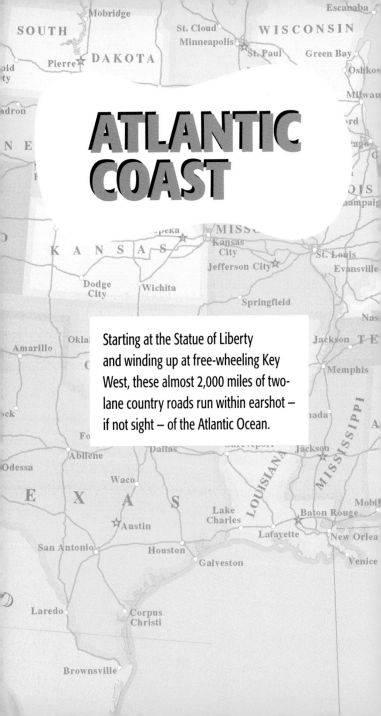

ATLANTIC COAST

Starting at the Statue of Liberty and winding up at free-wheeling Key West, these almost 2,000 miles of two-lane country roads run within earshot — if not sight — of the Atlantic Ocean.

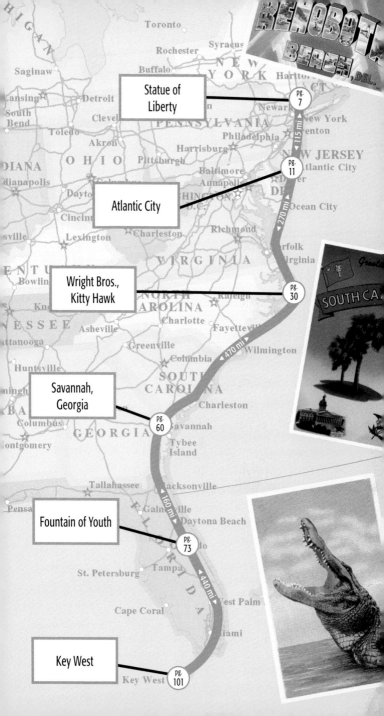

Statue of
Liberty

115 mi

Atlantic City

270 mi

Wright Bros.,
Kitty Hawk

470 mi

Savannah,
Georgia

Fountain of Youth

160 mi

Key West

440 mi

pg.
7

pg.
11

pg.
30

pg.
60

pg.
73

pg.
101

Between New York City and the Tip of Florida

If your impressions of the East Coast come from driving along the I-95 corridor through nearly nonstop urban and industrial sprawl, following our Atlantic Coast route will open your eyes to a whole other world. Alternating between wildly differing beach resort areas and lengthy stretches of pristine coastal wilderness, the route runs along almost 2,000 miles of two-lane country roads, within earshot, if not sight, of the Atlantic Ocean almost the entire way. In place of the grimy concrete and soulless netherworld of the Interstate, this route passes through innumerable quirky seaside towns and timeless old fishing villages, interspersed with huge swaths of beaches, wetlands, and woodlands that have hardly changed since the first explorers laid eyes on them four centuries ago.

Starting in the north at that all-American icon, the **Statue of Liberty,** and winding up in the south at free-wheeling **Key West,** this route truly offers something for everyone. Those searching for photogenic lighthouses or beachcombing solitude will love the undeveloped and usually deserted strands that stretch for miles along the low-lying islands that make up most of the coast, much of which, as at **Assateague Island** or **Cape Hatteras,** has been protected as national seashore parks. In contrast, the many beach resorts that dot the in-between areas vary from the grand Victorian charms of Cape May to the funky old Coney Island–style attractions of **Ocean City, Maryland,** and **Myrtle Beach, South Carolina,** with their boardwalks full of roller coasters, wax museums, and saltwater taffy stands. And let's not forget the glitzy casino resorts of **Atlantic City.**

Alongside the contemporary attractions are many evocative historic sites, including such unique places as **Roanoke Island, North Carolina,** where the first English-speaking colony in North America vanished without a trace in 1587. Lying south of the Mason-Dixon Line for almost all of its length, the route also visits many important Civil War sites, including **Fort Sumter,** where the first shots were fired, and the vital naval battlegrounds at **Hampton Roads** at the mouth of Chesapeake Bay. Midway along, we also pass one of the key sites of modern history: the windy sand dunes at **Kitty Hawk** where the Wright Brothers first proved that humans could fly.

Though this Atlantic Coast route will bring you to many well-known sights, its real attraction is the traveling, stopping off for fried chicken or barbecue at one of the hundreds of roadside stands, watching the shrimp boats pull into a sleepy dock and unload their day's catch, or simply chatting with locals at the general store or post office in a town that may not even be on the map.

NEW JERSEY

Being so close to New York and Philadelphia, it's not surprising that New Jersey has among the busiest and most densely developed stretches of coastline in the country. It *is* surprising, however, that beyond the board-walk amusements and flashy gambling ca-sinos of **Atlantic City,** the New Jersey shore offers a whole lot more. As with most of the East Coast, the "shoreline" is actually a series of barrier islands separated from the mainland by wildlife-rich estuaries;

these provide fishing and bird-watching oppor-tunities, as well as a break from the ceaseless commercial and residential development along the ocean beaches. Bustling in summer, these beachfront communities—starting with **Margate** near Atlantic City, and running south through vi-brant **Wildwood** before winding up at the dainty Victorian-era beach resort of **Cape May**—offer something for every-one, all within a 150-mile stretch of shoreline.

The Statue of Liberty

Raising her lamp beside New York City's immense harbor, the **Statue of Liberty** is one of the most vivid emblems of America. Despite the fact she is French, given to the American people to celebrate the 100th anniversary of the Declaration

Inspired by the end of slavery following the Civil War, the Statue of Liberty took nearly 20 years to complete. Lady Liberty was sculpted in France, then the 300-plus pieces were put in crates and shipped across the ocean. The statue is just over 150 feet tall, but including her 150-foot stone pedestal, it was the tallest building in New York when dedicated in 1886.

New York City

Some people avoid New York City like the plague, but more than eight million others can't bear to leave the glorious buzzing mosaic that makes New York unique in the world. Love it or hate it, New York is New York, and this great metropolis is undeniably the capital of the capitalist world, with some of the best museums, the best shops, the best sights, and the best restaurants in the world.

There's not much point in our recommending a select few of New York's huge spectrum of attractions, so we'll get straight to offering some practical help. For drivers, to whom all roads must seem to converge upon—and become gridlocked in—New York City, if you value your sanity and your shock absorbers: park your car in a long-term lot (not on the streets; city parking regulations are arcane and the fines huge) and walk or take public transportation. New York's subway system, one of the most extensive in the world, is relatively safe and usually the fastest way to get around town; it's also inexpensive ($2.25 per ride, or $8 a day, payable via electronic Metrocard). City buses are generally slower, but you see more of the sights. Taxis are ubiquitous—except when you want one.

The key to a successful visit to New York City is finding a place to stay. Ideally, you'll have an expense account, a friend,

or a rich aunt, but lacking that, here are a few suggestions, most in the low-to-moderate range. It's hard to beat the **Holiday Inn Soho** ($225 and up; 212/966-8898) at 138 Lafayette Street for convenience, as it's equidistant from Chinatown, Little Italy, SoHo, and TriBeCa. For families, another good option is the **Embassy Suites,** 102 North End Avenue ($299 and up; 212/945-0100) at Battery Park City, with views of the Statue of Liberty. The least expensive place in town is the very large and popular **HI-New York Hostel** (212/932-2300), on the Upper West Side at 891 Amsterdam Avenue at 103rd Street, with private rooms (around $75) plus dorm beds for less than $40 a night. One of the many fabulous hotels in New York City is the small, stylish, and recently renovated Ian Shrager hotel, **Morgans** ($299 and up; 212/686-0300) at 237 Madison Avenue.

Eating out is another way to blow a lot of money very quickly, but there are some great places where you can get both a good meal and a feel for New York without going bankrupt. One such place is **Katz's Delicatessen,** 205 E. Houston Street (212/254-2246), a Lower East Side landmark that's been serving up man-sized sandwiches (including great pastrami) since 1888. (For movie buffs, Katz's is where Meg Ryan did her famous fake-orgasm scene in When Harry Met Sally.) And if you like diners, check out the **Empire Diner** (212/243-2736), at 210 10th Avenue at 22nd Street in the Chelsea neighborhood—all black enamel and gleaming stainless steel, and open 24 hours, 7 days a week. Another affordable all-American experience can be had at the retro-trendy **Shake Shack,** a high-style burger stand with two branches: outdoors in Madison Square Park, a leafy oasis off Madison Avenue at E. 23rd Street (212/889-6600), and on the Upper West Side near the Museum of Natural History at 366 Columbus Avenue (646/747-8770). On the Upper East Side, between the Metropolitan and Whitney museums, Michelin-starred chef Daniel Boulud serves up exquisitely prepared French bistro fare at his **Cafe Boulud,** 20 E. 76th Street (212/772-2600). The ever-changing menu features a wide variety of traditional favorites and contemporary inventions, available for lunch and dinner at (comparatively) moderate prices. It's very popular, so make reservations as soon as you can.

of Independence, the statue has come to symbolize the Land of the Free and the Home of the Brave. Its spirit has long been evoked by the poem Emma Lazarus wrote in 1883 to help raise funds for installing the Statue of Liberty. Called "New Colossus," the poem ends with these famous words:

Keep ancient lands, your storied pomp!" cries she
With silent lips. "Give me your tired, your poor,
Your huddled masses yearning to breathe free,
The wretched refuse of your teeming shore.
Send these, the homeless, tempest-tost to me,
I lift my lamp beside the golden door!"

The Statue of Liberty sits on a 12-acre island and can be visited by ferry only (daily; $12; 877/LADY-TIX). It's about a mile from Manhattan, but much easier to reach from **Liberty State Park** in Jersey City, off New Jersey Turnpike exit 14B. (Both ferry routes also visit Ellis Island, where some 12 million immigrants entered the United States.) There is no admission fee for the Statue of Liberty, but if you want to climb up onto the "pedestal" you need a free, time-stamped "monument pass," which you can get when you buy the ferry tickets.

All pass-holders can explore the base of the Statue of Liberty and gaze up inside her hollow shell, but access up into the very small viewing area in the crown on her head requires special tickets ($3 extra), and a climb up more than 350 steps; her torch has been off-limits since 1916. In the security-conscious environment, the welcoming sentiments expressed in the Lazarus poem can seem quite sharply ironic, and sadly, the experience of visiting the statue can end up having more to do with restrictions and limitations than it does with grand concepts like "Liberty."

The New Jersey Shore

The northernmost stretches of the New Jersey shore are not exactly appetizing, and visitors bound for the beaches and vacation spots farther south turn a blind eye to the industrial blight. From **Perth Amboy** (Vaseline) to **Asbury Park** (Bruce Springsteen), the region has given the world many distinctive products, and there are a couple of intriguing Victorian-era resorts like **Spring Lake** and **Avon-by-the-Sea,** but to be honest, the attractions increase the farther south you go.

The middle stretch of the Jersey shore is actually the quietest, with the million-acre **Pinelands National Preserve** covering the inland area with forest and wetlands, and the coastal **Long Beach Island** dotted with sleepy little fishing and retirement communities. The biggest sight hereabouts is at the northern tip of the island: **Barnegat Lighthouse** (daily; free; 609/494-2016), "Old Barney," whose image appears on personalized New Jersey license plates.

Atlantic City

Midway along the Jersey Shore, the world-famous beach resort of **Atlantic City** (pop. 39,958) has ridden the ups and downs of history. Home of the world's oldest beachfront boardwalk and the first pleasure pier, Atlantic City also spawned the picture postcard and the Miss America beauty contest. Perhaps most significant of all, the street names for

Monopoly were taken from Atlantic City, although the city's layout bears little resemblance to the board game (and there's no "Get Out of Jail Free" card, either).

Atlantic City reached its peak at the turn of the 20th century, when thousands of city-dwellers flocked here from New York and Philadelphia each weekend. Later on, as automobiles and airplanes brought better beaches and more exotic locales within reach, Atlantic City went into a half century of decline until **gambling** was legalized in the 1970s and millions of dollars flowed into the local economy from speculating real-estate developers like Donald Trump, whose name is emblazoned on a number of towering resort hotels. These days, the boardwalk of Atlantic City has been transformed from a derelict relic into a glitzy gambling resort, attracting some 35 million annual visitors and millions of dollars daily to its casinos. It's no Las Vegas, and the population is still comparatively poor and shrinking, but the clattering of slot machines and the buzz of the craps tables continues 24 hours a day year-round.

The **Boardwalk,** backed by a wall of 25-story casino/hotels, is still the main focus of Atlantic City, running along the beach for over two miles. Few of the remaining pleasure piers offer much of interest, and only the rebuilt **Steel Pier,** located opposite Trump's Taj Mahal, holds the traditional seaside rides and arcade games, plus a sometimes-lively branch of the House of Blues nightclub chain.

Besides constituting Atlantic City's main attractions, the casinos hold most of the places to eat, apart from the dozens of fast-food stands along the Boardwalk. That said, a couple of old

To enjoy a day on the sands at many of New Jersey's beaches, you need to buy (and wear) a beach badge, which costs around $2 a day and is available at local tourist offices, shops, and fast-food stands.

favorites stand out from the seedy crowd of ramshackle businesses that fill the nearby streets. One is the birthplace of the "submarine" sandwich, the chrome **White House Sub Shop** (609/345-1564), open until midnight every day at 2301 Arctic Avenue. A block away, but at the other end of the aesthetic and budgetary spectrum, is **Dock's Oyster House** (609/345-0092) at 2405 Atlantic Avenue, a white-linen, dinner-only restaurant that's been serving great seafood since 1871. Along with a number of national chains, the casinos also control accommodation options—expect to pay upwards of $150 a night, though off-peak bargains can be found.

To take the pulse of the Jersey shore's nightlife, tune to **WZXL 100.7 FM,** which advertises nightly events and plays a proven mix of alternative rock hits, from Lou Reed to R.E.M.

Margate: Lucy the Elephant

Immediately south of Atlantic City, tidy **Margate** (pop. 8,400) fans out along the shore, its solidly suburban streets lined by grand houses. Margate utterly lacks the reckless seaside qualities of its larger neighbor, but does include one classic remnant of the Jersey shore's glory days: **Lucy the Elephant** (daily in summer, limited hours rest of the year; $6; 609/823-6473). The six-story wood-and-tin pachyderm, a curiosity built by a Philadelphia real-estate speculator in the 1880s to draw customers to his newly laid-out community, looms over the beach at 9200 Atlantic Avenue. The landmark architectural folly was used around the turn of the 20th century as a tavern and now holds a small museum of local history. Visitors walk through the museum on the way up to an observation deck, which is disguised as a canopied seat on Lucy's back.

Saved from demolition and restored by community efforts in the 1970s, Lucy is ever in need of repair, kept alive by tour monies, donations, and sales of Lucy souvenirs in the small gift shop.

Ocean Drive: Ocean City and Stone Harbor

A series of local roads collectively known as Ocean Drive runs along the south Jersey coast, passing through a number of family-oriented beach resorts, starting at Ocean City, "The Greatest Family Resort for a Vacation, or a Lifetime," 10 miles south of Atlantic City. **Ocean City** (pop. 15,500) was founded as a religious retreat in the late 1870s, and hasn't strayed far from its roots: Every summer morning (at 9:20 AM, on the dot), life on the Boardwalk promenade comes to a standstill as "The Star-Spangled Banner" blares out from loudspeakers and the American flag is raised at the beachfront amusement park. Located at 6th Street, and known as **Gillian's Wonderland Pier** (daily in summer, weekends only spring and fall; free admission, fee per ride; 609/399-7082), this old-time funfair has over 30 rides, including a giant Ferris wheel and a 1920s carousel. A block south, you can cool off on a hot summer's day at **Gillian's Island** water park.

Vacation homes, marinas, miniature golf courses, and a pair of toll bridges mark Ocean Drive for the next 20 miles. At **Stone Harbor,** five miles north of Wildwood, the **Wetlands Institute** (daily in summer, Tues.–Sat. rest of year; $7; 609/368-1211), at 1075 Stone Harbor Boulevard, is one of the best places to experience the abundant natural life of the New Jersey shore. An observation tower looking over 6,000 acres of saltwater marshland provides excellent bird-watching opportunities, and there's also a museum with a touch-tank and aquarium.

Wildwood

On the Jersey Shore, fun in the sun reaches a peak at raucous **Wildwood,** a trio of interconnected towns housing dozens of nightclubs and New Jersey's biggest beachfront amusement parks. The largest of all, **Mariners Landing** on the pier at Schellenger Avenue, has 35 rides including the largest Ferris wheel on the East Coast. At 25th Street is **Morey's Pier,** which has a miniature golf course that takes you through the history of the New Jersey shore. A little farther south is **Morey's**

Adventure Pier, which is home to the "Great White," the only wooden roller coaster in the U.S. to be built on a pier. All three of these are owned by the Morey family, prime movers behind Wildwood's retro-rediscovery, and an all-ride, all-pier pass (around $50; 609/522-3900) is available for a full day's fun.

Away from the sands in the low-key downtown district at 3907 Pacific Avenue, Wildwood's local history **museum** (free; 609/523-0277) is worth a look for its one unique feature: the **National Marbles Hall of Fame,** featuring thousands of glass balls and more marble-shooting paraphernalia than you've ever seen. The museum, which hosts the National Marbles Championship every June, also has a fascinating and informative display of postcards, documenting the region's recent past.

For many visitors, the best reason to spend time in Wildwood is that the area boasts an extensive collection of 1950s roadside architecture—mainly motel after motel, all sporting exuberant Las Vegas–style neon signs. Many of these motels are closed in the November–May off-season, but in the warmer months you can step back in the past by staying the night in one of these classic "Doo Wop" motels—like the **Mango Motel** (609/522-2067) at 209 E. Spicer Avenue, or the renovated **Lollipop Motel** (609/729-2800) at 2300 Atlantic Avenue. Or just stop for a meal at the chrome-and-glass **Pink Cadillac Diner** (609/522-8288), a block south of the main pier at 3801 Atlantic Avenue.

For more details on places to stay and things to do—like October's massive and rowdy **Thunder on the Beach** monster truck rally—contact the **Wildwood visitors center,** 3601 Boardwalk (800/992-9732).

Cape May

A world away from the carnival atmosphere of the Wildwoods, **Cape May,** the oldest and most serene of the New Jersey beach towns, sits at the southern tip of the state. First settled in the early 1600s, Cape May's glory years ran from the 1850s to the 1890s as an upper-crust summer resort, when it rivaled Newport, Rhode Island, as the destination of choice for the power brokers of Philadelphia and New York City.

A few modern motels and miniature golf courses spread along Cape May's broad beaches, while the compact downtown district retains all its overwrought Victorian splendor. Century-old cottages now house cafés, boutiques, and art galleries, and it seems as if every other building has been converted into a quaint B&B. The town's ornate gingerbread mansions were constructed in the aftermath of a disastrous 1878 fire; among the better examples is the elaborate **Emlen Physick House,** eight blocks north of downtown at 1048 Washington Street, designed by noted Philadelphia architect Frank Furness. It now houses the nonprofit, preservation-oriented **Mid-Atlantic Center for the**

Cape May–Lewes Ferry

Running between the tip of the New Jersey shore and the heart of the Delaware coast, the Cape May–Lewes Ferry carries cars and passengers on a relaxing ride across the mouth of Delaware Bay. The trip costs about $30 for a car and one passenger, plus fees for each additional passenger. Schedules change seasonally, with boats leaving about every two hours in summer and every three hours in winter. Crossings take about 90 minutes, and if the seas are calm you can often see porpoises playing in the swells.

For up-to-date times and other information, call 800/643-3779. Reservations ($5 extra) are a very good idea at peak travel times and should be made at least one day in advance.

Arts and is open as a museum of late Victorian life (daily in summer, weekends only in winter; $8; 609/884-5404).

Pick up walking-tour maps of some of the town's 600 listed historic buildings, and do a taste-test of Cape May's many architecturally magnificent, mostly Victorian-era **bed-and-breakfasts.** These include the mansard-roofed **Queen Victoria** ($150 and up; 609/884-8702) at 102 Ocean Street, and the **Mainstay Inn** ($175 and up; 609/884-8690) at 635 Columbia Avenue, which has a spacious veranda opening onto gorgeous gardens. Cape May's oldest and most atmospheric place to stay is the Southern gothic **Chalfonte Hotel** ($80–140; 609/884-8409), located at 301 Howard Street. What the Chalfonte lacks in TVs, telephones, and air-conditioning, it more than makes up for in hospitality: a bank of front porch rocking chairs, full breakfasts, and huge, down-home dinners are all included in the rates.

Places to eat, including a dozen or so bakeries, cafés, restaurants, and bars, can be found along the pedestrian-friendly few blocks of Washington Street at the center of town, while the best seafood restaurants, naturally enough, are near the marina and ferry terminal on the north edge of town, off US-9. One more great option for a hearty all-American breakfast or a Greek-inflected lunch: **George's Place,** right downtown, on the water at 301 Beach Drive (609/884-6088).

DELAWARE

Across Delaware Bay from Cape May, the Delaware shore is considerably quieter and more peaceful than New Jersey's. Both shores, originally settled by Scandinavian whalers who established port colonies here in the early 1600s, share a common history. But because the Delaware shore is that much farther from the urban centers, it has been spared the overdevelopment of much of the rest of the coast. Nevertheless, Delaware's statewide population of half a million doubles in summer as visitors from Baltimore and Washington, D.C., descend upon its coastal resorts, from historic **Lewes** to lively **Rehoboth Beach** to the untouched sands of **Delaware Seashore State Park,** stretching south to the Maryland border.

Lewes and Cape Henlopen

Sitting at the southern lip of Delaware Bay, **Lewes** is a sportfishing center that traces its roots back to 1631, when it was settled by the Dutch West India Company as a whaling port. Though this colony lasted only two years, Lewes calls itself the "First Town in the First State," commemorating its history in the false-gabled brick **Zwannendael Museum** at the center of town (closed Mon.; free).

Zwannendael Museum

Lewes also harbors huge sand dunes, a fine stretch of beach, and a **campground** with showers in 3,000-acre **Cape Henlopen State Park,** east of town at the mouth of Delaware Bay. Expect relative peace and quiet here, since most visitors, arriving off the Cape May ferry, simply rush through Lewes to the beach resorts farther south. Serving three meals a day, the best food is at the **Blue Plate Diner** (302/644-8400), near the ferry terminal at 329 Savannah Road.

Rehoboth Beach

Fronting the open Atlantic, **Rehoboth Beach** was founded in the 1870s when church groups bought beachfront land, established the town, and extended a railroad line south from Lewes. The highway frontage along Hwy-1 is over-full of franchise food and factory outlet malls, but the heart of town along Rehoboth Avenue is the place to go. With its small but lively Sputnik-era **Funland Amusement Park,** where the rides include bumper cars and a nighttime haunted house, and a tidy boardwalk running along the broad beach, Rehoboth has somehow retained a small-town feel despite the many thousands of bureaucrats and power brokers who descend upon the place during the summer, escaping the sweltering heat of Washington, D.C.

The D.C. connection helps explain the town's profusion of very good (and some very expensive) restaurants. Lining the main drag are casual, kid-friendly places like **Dogfish Head** (302/226-BREW) at 320 Rehoboth Avenue, which has great food and killer beers in Delaware's oldest microbrewery. More grown-up palates will be drawn to the gourmet places a block south, where the outrageously kitsch **La La Land** (302/227-3887) at 22 Wilmington Avenue fills a pair of old beach houses alongside the eclectic, Mediterranean-inspired and unfailingly yummy **Espuma** (302/227-4199) at 28 Wilmington Avenue. There are also the more mainstream delights of **Thrashers French Fries,** and sundry beer-and-burger stands along the Boardwalk.

Places to stay include some quaint old B&Bs and a barrage of highway chain motels, plus local ones like the **Beach View** ($150; 800/288-5962), on the boardwalk at 6 Wilmington Avenue.

Ever wonder what happens to all those pumpkins that don't get bought by Halloween? In Delaware, they end up as fodder for a unique competition, the **Punkin' Chunkin',** in which the helpless gourds get launched hundreds, even thousands of feet through the air by a variety of mechanical devices. Thousands turn out for the event, which is usually held the first weekend in November; for details, call 302/856-1444.

Delaware Seashore State Park

South from Rehoboth stretches one of the last, long stretches of pristine beach on the whole northern East Coast: **Delaware Seashore State Park** (302/227-3071), which contains six miles of open beach with golden-flecked white sand and acres of marshland estuary, thronged in season with migrating birds—and bird-watchers (and campers and anglers, too.) The park's many beaches are all easily accessible from beachfront Hwy-1.

The park has camping and nice new cottages (costing $1,500 a week in summer!) and is book-ended by a pair of densely developed resort towns: **Dewey Beach** in the north draws a younger, collegiate crowd, while **Bethany Beach** in the south attracts more families.

Approaching Maryland, the 1858 **Fenwick Island**

Lighthouse, on the bay side of Hwy-1 just south of Hwy-54, marks the state border. This lighthouse is a local landmark, but the waist-high white marker in front of it may be more significant: Placed in 1751, it marked the boundary between Maryland and Pennsylvania, of which Delaware was then a part. Showing respect to the colonial proprietors, the more than 250-year-old marker has the Calvert Family coat of arms on the Maryland (south) side, and William Penn's family crest on the other.

MARYLAND

Maryland, the most oddly shaped of the lower 48 states, shares the broad "DelMarVa" peninsula with Delaware and a small piece of Virginia. The inland area along the eastern shore of Chesapeake Bay,

with its many inlets and tributary rivers, is filled with dozens of small colonial-era towns and fishing villages, while the Atlantic Coast is completely taken up by two very different beasts: the gloriously kitschy beach resort of **Ocean City** and the untrammeled wilds of **Assateague Island National Seashore.** Heading inland around Assateague, the highway passes by a number of historic small towns, including **Berlin** and captivating **Snow Hill.**

Ocean City

About the only place left on the entire East Coast that retains the carnival qualities of classic seaside resorts, **Ocean City** (pop. 7,173, swelling to some 400,000 in summer) has by far the best array of old-time funfair attractions in the Mid-Atlantic (well, south of Wildwood, New Jersey, at least). On and around the main **Ocean Pier** at the south end of the island, there are enough merry-go-rounds, Ferris wheels, roller coasters (including "The Hurricane," which is illustrated with scenes from Ocean City storms past), mini-golf courses, haunted houses, and bumper cars to divert a small army. A block in-

To go along with its great beaches, Ocean City has a radio station, the excellent **WOCM 98.1 FM,** playing classic rock 'n' roll and broadcasting details of Ocean City's nightclub scene.

land, **Trimper's Amusements,** in business since the 1890s, has two more roller coasters, plus a Tilt-a-Whirl, a 100-year-old Hershell carousel, and a spooky haunted house. Come while you can—places like Trimpers are threatened by rising property values (and property taxes) and are increasingly close to becoming extinct.

From the pier north, Ocean City stretches for over two miles along a broad, clean, white-sand beach. A wide, part-wooden boardwalk lines the sands, packed with arcades full of video games and a few nearly forgotten old amusements like skee-ball and pokerino, not to mention midway contests—the kind where, for $1 a try, you can win stuffed animals and other prizes by shooting baskets or squirting water into clowns' mouths. A ramshackle collection of fortune-tellers, T-shirt stands, and burger-and-beer bars completes the scene, forming a busy gauntlet that is among the nation's liveliest promenades.

On summer weekends, Ocean City becomes Maryland's second-largest city, and most of the fun is simply in getting

caught up in the garish human spectacle of it all, but there are a couple of specific things worth searching out. For the price of a bumper car ride, you can enjoy the quirky collections of the **Life-Saving Station Museum** (daily May–Oct., weekends only in winter; $3), at the south end of the boardwalk, where alongside displays of shipwrecks and bathing suits you can compare and contrast bowls full of sand from 100 different beaches around the world. The museum also marks the starting point for the open-air **trams** ($3) that run north along the boardwalk for over two miles.

Much of Ocean City's charm is decidedly lowbrow,

but the **food** is better than you might expect, with numerous places offering plates full of shrimp and pitchers of beer for under $10, and fresh-fried chicken or crab cakes available from boardwalk stands. **Thrashers Fries** are available (no ketchup; salt and vinegar only!) from a number of counters along the boardwalk, and you can top them off with a cone or milk shake from **Dumser's Ice Cream,** near the Wax Museum at the south end of the boardwalk.

Places to stay are also abundant, though many of the huge concrete towers you see are actually condominiums and not available for overnight stays. In fact, of all the dozen or more grand, older hotels, only the **Atlantic Hotel** ($80 and up; 410/289-9111 or 800/328-5268), on the oceanfront at Wicomico Street, is still open for business. Modern motels like the **Oceanic** (410/289-6494), looking across the inlet to Assateague Island from 710 S. Philadelphia Street, charge as much as $200 a night for a room that goes for less than $50 off-season.

For complete listings of lodgings and restaurants, contact the **Ocean City visitors center** (410/289-2800 or 800/OC-OCEAN), in the Convention Center at 4001 Coastal Highway.

Assateague Island National Seashore

At one time, Assateague Island, the long thin barrier island on which Ocean City sits, stretched in an unbroken line all the way into Virginia. In 1933, a major storm crashed through the sands and created the broad inlet that now divides Ocean City from the near-wilderness of **Assateague Island National Seashore.** One of the few areas of the Atlantic coast protected from commercial development, Assateague Island offers some 37 miles and 10,000 acres of hiking, swimming, camping, canoeing, bicycling, clamming, and bird-watching. Swarms of voracious mosquitoes and a lack of fresh water keep the crowds to a minimum.

To reach the island from Ocean City, follow US-50 west for two miles and turn south on Hwy-611, which loops around Sinexpunt Bay before arriving at the **visitors center** (daily; 410/641-1441). The center has a small aquarium as well as maps, guides, and up-to-date information about the national seashore.

On the road between Ocean City and Assateague Island, at the junction of US-50 and Hwy-611, the very nice **Wheels**

of Yesterday vehicle museum ($4; 410/213-7329) displays more than 30 classic cars and trucks and has a great little gift shop too.

Berlin and Snow Hill

From Ocean City, the route turns inland around Assateague Island and Chincoteague Bay, following US-50 west for eight miles, then turning south on US-113 through the dark cypress swamps along the Pocomoke River. Just southwest of the US-50/113 junction, the remarkably well-preserved town of **Berlin** offers a look back at a slower-paced era. Redbrick buildings house antique shops around the 1890s landmark **Atlantic Hotel** ($95 and up; 410/641-3589) at 2 N. Main Street, where the row of rocking chairs along the open-air front porch all but demand that you sit and stay a while. Inside, the stylish Solstice bistro may tempt you to alter your travel plans so you can enjoy the delicious local seafood.

Another 15 miles southwest of Ocean City, detour west from the highway to take a look at the 250-year-old town of **Snow Hill** (pop. 2,200). The **Julia A. Purnell Museum** (Tues.–Sun. April–Nov. only; $2), housed in an old church at 208 W. Market Street, features a range of exhibits tracing Eastern Shore history. Pick up a walking-tour map of Snow Hill's many significant structures, or if the weather's fine, paddle a canoe through the surrounding wild cypress swamps with the **Pocomoke River Canoe Company** (410/632-3971), at 312 N. Washington Street, next to the drawbridge.

VIRGINIA

Virginia's Eastern Shore is among the most isolated regions of the country, and its dozens of small towns and villages remain much as they have for centuries. Everything on the Eastern Shore is on a much smaller scale than on the mainland, and the many stands selling fresh corn and tomatoes along the roadside attest to the important role farming plays in the local economy. Although fast-food places, chicken-processing plants, and a couple of modern malls dot US-13, the main route through Virginia's Eastern Shore, the area is still mostly rural and undeveloped, with business loops turning off through the many well-preserved old towns. The numerous historic sites include colonial-era plantations and archaeological remnants of Native American tribes.

The highlight for most visitors is **Chincoteague,** a small commercial and sportfishing port sitting at the entrance to massive **Chincoteague National Wildlife Refuge,** which faces the Atlantic Coast and offers the only ocean beaches in this part of the state. South of Chincoteague, US-13 runs down the center of the narrow Eastern Shore peninsula, giving access to the Chesapeake Bay waterfront at **Onancock,** then passing through numerous small towns like **Accomac** and **Eastville,** neither of which has changed much since Revolutionary times.

Crossing the mouth of the Chesapeake Bay via a 23-mile-long bridge and tunnel brings you to maritime Norfolk and the state's main Atlantic resort, Virginia Beach, before the route turns inland and south into North Carolina.

Chincoteague

The drive into **Chincoteague** (pop. 4,317; SCHINK-a-teeg), a low-key fishing village, takes you across miles of glowing gold and blue marshlands through a gauntlet of quirky billboards advertising local motels, restaurants, and sportfishing charters. This mix of natural beauty and tacky tourism aptly reflects the character of the town, which is totally dependent upon summertime visitors but seems to wish that we'd all just leave and let the locals go fishing.

A small bridge along Hwy-175, which runs 10 miles east from US-17, drops you at the heart of town, where casual seafood restaurants line the small wharves that stretch along the bay. For breakfast, head south of town to the end of Ridge Road, where the popular **Island Family** (757/336-1198) serves up hearty meals across from the "pony swim" landing.

In summer, stands selling fresh fruit and vegetables—particularly sweet corn and tomatoes—dot roadsides all over the Eastern Shore.

Among the many places to stay are several nice B&Bs and a handful of standard motels like the friendly and central **Birchwood** ($65 and up; 757/336-6133) at 3650 N. Main Street.

Chincoteague National Wildlife Refuge

The **Chincoteague National Wildlife Refuge** is one of the largest nature preserves along the Atlantic flyway, attracting hundreds of species of birds, including egrets, herons, geese, swans, and snow geese, not to mention thousands and thousands of migrating ducks. A continuation of the Assateague Island National Seashore across the Maryland border, the refuge contains hundreds of acres of marshland, excellent beaches, and a number of hiking and cycling trails. The refuge **visitors center** (daily; 757/336-6122) has detailed information on park activities as well as special exhibits on Chincoteague's famous **wild ponies,** which can usually be seen from the Woodland Trail that loops south from Beach Road.

The children's story **Misty of Chincoteague** is set in the area and tells how wild ponies—whose ancestors were sent here by English settlers in the late 1600s—are rounded up from the wildlife refuge on Assateague Island for a forced swim across to Chincoteague. The annual roundup, swim, and auction benefits local firefighters and attracts thousands of spectators. The swim takes place the last Wednesday in July, and the auction follows the next day.

South of town at the end of Main Street, just outside the refuge boundary, you can pitch a tent or park an RV at the privately owned **Tom's Cove Campground** (757/336-6498).

Accomac

One of the most photogenic spots on the Eastern Shore,

Accomac (pop. 547) is centered on an ancient-looking red-brick courthouse, flanked by a series of wooden sheds converted into professional offices. The old library next door dates from the 1780s and was used for years as a debtor's prison; the library, courthouse, and surrounding buildings make up one of the more extensive collections of colonial-era buildings in the country. By way of contrast, Accomac is also home to a huge Perdue Chicken processing plant, right along US-13.

Onancock and Tangier Island

The picturesque harbor town of **Onancock** (pop. 1,525, o-NAN-cock), on the Chesapeake Bay two miles west of US-13 via Hwy-179, is one of the nicest towns on the Eastern Shore. A short walking tour of over a dozen historical homes and churches begins at perhaps the finest mansion on the Eastern Shore, the **Kerr Place** (Tues.–Sat. 10 AM–4 PM; $5; 757/787-8012) at 69 Market Street, built in 1799 and now home to the offices and museum of the Eastern Shore Historical Society. Another historic curiosity is the 150-year-old Hopkins and Bros. General Store, on the wharf at 2 Market Street, which in the past has sold everything from sweet potatoes to postcards—and now serves as a sort of mini welcome center. A great taste of Onancock life awaits inside the **Corner Bakery** (757/787-4520), at 36 Market Street, where great doughnuts and fresh coffee are served up to a mostly local crowd, or in the evening you can catch a flick at Onancock's nifty 1950s movie theater, the **Roseland** (757/787-2209) on Market Street.

Onancock was born and grew up around its natural deep-water harbor, and the town wharf is still the place to catch the seasonal ferry across Chesapeake Bay to **Tangier Island,** an evocative old place where things seem to have hardly changed since colonial times. The few hundred people who live here year-round have a unique and almost indecipherably archaic accent—which some trace back to 17th-century Cornwall, England—and earn their livelihoods catching crabs and the occasional oyster from Chesapeake Bay. Tangier Island is best known for its soft-shell crabs, which are sold all over the eastern United States.

Visiting Tangier Island is easy, but takes some advance planning. From mid-April until October, boats leave once a day from Onancock Wharf (about $35; 757/891-2240); travel time is one hour and 15 minutes each way, leaving around 10 AM and returning around 3 PM. This means visitors returning on the ferry have only about two hours on the island, so staying over-night at a homespun B&B like **Shirley's Bay View Inn** (757/891-2396) or **Hilda Crockett's Chesapeake House** (757/891-2331) is about the only way to have any kind of close encounter with the tourist-shy locals. Hilda's also serves meals, and good seafood can be had at a handful of unpretentious places like the **Fisherman's Corner Restaurant** (757/891-2900), where you may well be served by the person who caught your meal (or his sister).

Bike rentals are available on Tangier Island, no part of which of which is more than five feet above sea level.

Eastville

You can get a good idea of just how rural and quiet life is on Virginia's Eastern Shore by visiting **Eastville** (pop. 185), the seat of Northampton County. A mile west of US-13 on a well-marked business loop, Eastville centers on the red-brick courthouse and old county jail, with a handful of even older buildings dating back to the mid-1700s. Eastville has an excellent roadside crab shack along US-13: the **Great Machipongo Clam Shack** (757/442-3800) has crabmeat sandwiches, fresh steamed clams, and an aston-ishing variety of shellfish, most of it grown, caught, or picked by the owners.

Chesapeake Bay Bridge/Tunnel

One of the more impressive engineering feats on the East Coast is the **Chesapeake Bay Bridge/Tunnel,** which opened in 1964 at the mouth of the Chesapeake Bay and was effectively doubled in 1997 by the addition of an extra set of driving lanes. Almost 18 miles long and charging a $12 toll, the structure consists of one high-level bridge, two deep tunnels, four islands, and many miles of raised causeway. Two miles from the southern end of the bridge, a fishing pier and restaurant operate on man-made Sea Gull Island.

Before the Chesapeake Bay Bridge/Tunnel was completed in 1964, ferries linking the Eastern Shore with the mainland docked at **Cape Charles,** west of US-13 eight miles south of Eastville. Barges still use the harbor, ferrying freight trains across the bay.

Virginia Beach

From the toll plaza at the southern end

of the Chesapeake Bay Bridge, US-60 heads east along Atlantic Avenue, passing through the woodland waterfront of **First Landing State Park** before winding up at the ocean and **Virginia Beach** (pop. 435,000), the state's most populous (and fastest-growing) city, and its one and only beach resort. Ten-story hotels line the main drag, Atlantic Avenue, which is plastered with large signs banning cars from "cruising" the mile-long array of funfairs, surf shops, and nightclubs.

The two deepwater harbors near Norfolk at the mouth of the Chesapeake Bay, **Newport News** and **Hampton Roads,** are the headquarters of the U.S. Navy's Atlantic Fleet and together form the world's largest naval base.

Unlike many coastal towns, Virginia Beach also boasts a significant history. Virginia's first colonists landed at Virginia Beach on April 26, 1607, before settling upriver at Jamestown; the site is marked by a stone cross at Cape Henry, at the southern lip of Chesapeake Bay. Five miles south, the excellent **Virginia Marine Sciences Museum,** 717 General Booth Boulevard (daily; $12; 757/385-FISH), has nearly a million gallons of sharks, sting rays, barracudas, and sea turtles, and an IMAX theater ($8–12 extra).

If you see or hear warnings about **shark attacks,** take them seriously. In recent years many swimmers have been badly injured or killed by sharks, even in very shallow water.

Dining options tend toward seafood restaurants hidden away in the resort hotels, though the **Maple Tree Pancake House** (757/425-6796), at 2608 Atlantic Avenue, is a great breakfast stop. The **Jewish Mother** (757/422-5430) at 3108 Pacific Avenue serves up good salads and huge deli sandwiches, and it doubles as a popular nightclub.

Perhaps the best reason to stop at Virginia Beach is that accommodations are much cheaper here than out on the Outer Banks: Dorm beds at **Angie's Guest Cottage HI Hostel** (757/428-4690) at 302 24th Street cost around $20 a night. There are a few locally run places, like the **Golden Sands Inn** ($80–130; 757/428-1770), at 1312 Atlantic Avenue, and campers will appreciate the fine facilities at **First Landing State Park** (757/412-2300).

Virginia Beach is home to the **Association for Research and Enlightenment** (800/333-4499), at 67th and Atlantic, which is dedicated to continuing the legacy of early American psychic Edgar Cayce, offering classes in ESP—but you already knew that, didn't you?

Norfolk

During colonial times, **Norfolk** (pop. 234,403; NAW-fik)

was the largest city in Virginia and one of the busiest ports in North America. It's still very much connected with the water, which you can experience firsthand at the **Nauticus National Maritime Center** (daily in summer, closed Mon. rest of year; $19; 757/664-1000), where the engaging displays inside are dwarfed by the massive hulk of the battleship USS *Wisconsin* moored alongside. Away from the waterfront, Norfolk has a couple more worthwhile destinations, including the lovely **Chrysler Museum** (Wed.–Sun.; $7; 757/664-6200), on the north side of downtown off Olney Road and Duke Street. The personal art collection of Walter Chrysler, the self-educated engineer who created one of the "Big Three" car companies and built New York's Chrysler Building, is displayed inside a commodious Italianate building. Norfolk, a staunch Navy town, also holds the final resting place of controversial U.S. Army Gen. Douglas MacArthur, preserved alongside his personal papers (and his 1950 Chrysler Imperial limousine) at the **MacArthur Memorial** (daily; free), inside Norfolk's old City Hall building at Bank and Plume Streets downtown.

The **Norfolk Tides** (757/622-2222), Class AAA farm team of the Baltimore Orioles, play at beautiful Harbor Park, off I-264 at Waterside Drive, where you can watch big ships sail past.

Even if you're just racing through, bound for the beach, Norfolk has one place where you really ought to stop and eat: **Doumar's Cones and BBQ** (757/627-4163), a half mile north of downtown at 19th Street and Monticello Avenue. Besides being a real old-fashioned drive-in, this place stakes a claim to having invented the ice cream cone, since the owner's uncle, Abe Doumar, sold the first ones at the 1904

Stop for a bite at Doumar's.

St. Louis World's Fair. Doumar's still sells great handmade cones, very good BBQ sandwiches, and a thirst-quenching limeade. Pass by at your peril. . . .

From Norfolk, you can take US-17 south across the aptly named Great Dismal Swamp, or follow the faster Hwy-168, which takes you past a feast of roadside fruit stands, BBQ shacks, and junk shops, straight down to Kitty Hawk and the Outer Banks of North Carolina.

NORTH CAROLINA

Wild Atlantic beaches, a handful of tiny fishing villages, and some of the country's most significant historic sites make coastal North Carolina a great place to visit. A highlight for many vacationers is the **Outer Banks,** miles of barrier islands where busy resort towns like **Nags Head** contrast with the stretches of pristine beaches protected on the **Cape Hatteras National Seashore.** Besides golden sands, the Outer Banks area includes two evocative historic sites: the dunes at **Kitty Hawk,** where the Wright Brothers first took to the air, and **Roanoke Island,** site of the first ill-fated English effort to colonize the New World. Farther south, beyond the quirky, small city of Wilmington, a movie-making mecca, the 300-mile coastal route turns inland around **Cape Fear,** heading toward the South Carolina border.

Kitty Hawk: The Wright Brothers National Memorial

Alternately known as Killy Hauk, Kitty Hock, and Killy Honk before its current name came into general use, **Kitty Hawk** to most people means one thing: the Wright Brothers' first powered airplane flight more than a century ago, on December 17, 1903. Lured by the steady winds that blow in from the Atlantic and by the high sand dunes that cover the shore, Wilbur and Orville Wright first came to the Outer Banks in 1900 and returned every year thereafter with prototype kites and gliders built out of bicycle parts, which they fine-tuned to create the world's first airplane. Their tale is truly one of the great adventure and success stories of the modern age, and the site of their experiments has been preserved as the **Wright Brothers National Memorial.** First stop is the **visitors center** (daily; $4; 252/473-2595), which includes a number of exhibits tracing the history of human efforts to fly. Every hour, rangers give engaging talks alongside a full-sized replica of the Wright Brothers' first plane.

Orville and Wilbur Wright

The most affecting aspect of the memorial is the unchanged site where the brothers first flew. Each of the first four flights is marked by stones set on the grassy field. The first flight, with Orville at the controls flying into a 25-mph headwind, lasted 12 seconds and covered just 120 feet—barely more than a brisk walking pace. The 90-foot-high sand dune where Wilbur and Orville first took to the air has been planted over with grasses to keep it from blowing away. A series of paths climbs to the top of the dune, where a 60-foot, wing-shaped granite pylon is inscribed with the words:

In commemoration of the conquest of the air by the brothers Wilbur and Orville Wright. Conceived by genius, achieved by dauntless resolution and unconquerable faith.

The park is off US-158, on the inland side of the highway, two miles south of the Wright Memorial Bridge from the mainland.

Though the memorial is definitely worth an extended visit, the towns around it are a bit disappointing—both Kitty Hawk and Kill Devil Hills are little more than narrow strips of commercial development.

Jockey's Ridge State Park

The windswept 110-foot-high twin sand dunes of **Jockey's Ridge State Park** (daily; free; 252/441-7132) tower over US-158 between Kitty Hawk and Nags Head. The highest sand dunes on the East Coast, Jockey's Ridge barely survived being bulldozed in the 1970s to form yet another Outer Banks resort; it's now one of the prime hang-gliding spots in the country—remember the Wright Brothers! Jockey's Ridge is also a nice place to wander the short boardwalk nature trail that points out the diverse plants and animals of the dune community. You may want to take your shoes off and scamper around the sands barefoot. If you feel especially daring, **Kitty Hawk Kites** across the highway at milepost 10.5 dubs itself the "World's Largest Hang-Gliding School" and offers equipment rentals and **lessons** ($90 and up; 252/441-4127 or 877/FLY-THIS), plus anything else you might need to make the most of your time here.

If you're traveling along the Carolina coast in summer, be aware that the **hurricane season** begins in June and lasts through the end of November. These are deadly serious storms, so take heed of any warnings, and follow the evacuation instructions broadcast over radio and TV networks.

Nags Head

The towns of the northern Outer Banks overlap each other so much it can be hard to tell you are in **Nags Head,** six miles south of Kitty Hawk. One of the oldest and most popular resorts in the region, Nags Head also offers the widest range of visitor facilities. Good places to spend a night or two include a beachfront roadside classic at Milepost 16.5: the historic **Sea Foam Motel** ($65–150; 252/441-7320), at 7111 S. Dare Trail, one of the last surviving 1940s motels on the Outer Banks. The pine-paneled walls, vivid tiles, and slamming screen doors will take you back to a simpler time. Nearby, the even more atmospheric **First Colony Inn** ($75–200; 252/441-2343),

The name Nags Head is derived from the practices of Outer Banks pirates, who tied lanterns around the heads of their horses to simulate boats bobbing at anchor. The lanterns lured passing ships onto shore, where they ran aground on the offshore sandbars.

The Outer Banks

The geography of the Outer Banks, a series of barrier islands stretching for over 200 miles along the coast of North Carolina, has changed dramatically over time, thanks to hurricanes and winter storms, not to mention human hands. Until a series of lighthouses was built beginning in the late 18th century, the islands and the offshore shoals were so treacherous they became known as the "Graveyard of the Atlantic."

Nowadays, the same places where pirates once plundered are given over to wind-surfing, hang-gliding, kite-surfing, sportfishing, and beachcombing, as the Outer Banks (sometimes abbreviated "OBX") have become a tourist and recreation destination par excellence. The resident population of some 30,000 swells to accommodate over six million annual visitors, but unlike its nearest comparison, Cape Cod, the Outer Banks area boasts only a few colonial towns. Instead, substantial development during the ongoing building boom has covered the sands with an ugly sprawl of vacation homes and time-share condos perched—often on stilts to protect them from storm damage—directly on the broad Atlantic beaches. Most of the development has taken place in the north along two parallel roads: US-158, usually called The Bypass but also known as Croatan Highway; and oceanfront Hwy-12, a.k.a. Virginia Dare Trail and Beach Road. Mileposts on both roads mark distances from north to south. There's plentiful lodging in the many little towns along Hwy-12; gas stations and fast-food restaurants line US-158. The exception to the commercial sprawl is the magical 75 miles of the Cape Hatteras National Seashore.

Along the northern Outer Banks, bridges link Nags Head and Kitty Hawk with the mainland, though access to the less-developed southern parts of the Outer Banks is limited to ferry boats, all of which carry cars.

along US-158 at milepost 16, was moved from its valuable oceanfront location to the middle of the island, but it still offers oodles of old-fashioned charm along with a delicious breakfast and afternoon tea.

One more long-standing local landmark, **Sam & Omie's** (252/441-7366), near the east end of US-64 at 7228 S. Virginia Dare Trail, has featured inexpensive but well-prepared family fare, three meals a day (plus a full bar), for over 70 years.

Roanoke Island: Fort Raleigh National Historic Site

From an area known as Whalebone Junction at the south end of Nags Head, US-64 runs west over a causeway and bridge to **Roanoke Island,** site of the first English settlement in North America. The legendary "Lost Colony" was first established in 1584 by Sir Walter Raleigh, but the effort was not a success, and the survivors returned to England. In 1587, a larger expedition of 110 colonists arrived, including 17 women and nine children, but because of the outbreak of war with Spain and the manifold difficulties involved in crossing the Atlantic Ocean, there was no further contact with England until 1590.

By the time the next supply ship returned, the settlers had disappeared without a trace, which prompted numerous theories about their fate. Now, amidst an eerily dark forest, the colony's original earthwork fortress has been excavated and reconstructed as the centerpiece of the **Fort Raleigh National Historic Site.** Exhibits inside the **visitors center** (daily; free; 252/473-5772) include a few rusty artifacts and dry displays explaining the historical context of the colonial effort. There are also copies of the many beautiful watercolors and drawings of native plants, animals, and people produced by the original expedition's two immensely talented scientists, John White and Thomas Hariot.

The historic port of **Manteo** (pop. 1,052; MAN-tee-o), in the middle of Roanoke Island between Fort Raleigh

Hundreds of ancient ships and unfortunate sailors met their watery end in the shallow waters off Cape Hatteras. The remains of over 2,000 vessels lie along the entire Carolina coastline; a few are visible from shore at low tide.

Throughout the summer, a waterfront theater adjacent to Fort Raleigh presents a popular production of *Lost Colony,* which dramatizes the events of the ill-fated settlement. Call for details or tickets ($16–20 adults, $8 under 11; 252/473-3414).

and the beach resorts of the Outer Banks, was named for the Native American who helped Sir Walter Raleigh and the Lost Colony. Manteo is the only county seat in North Carolina that's located on an island. You can still sense the town's proud seagoing history as you walk along the quiet streets near

Raleigh's flagship, *Ark Raleigh*

the tidied-up waterfront. Surrounded by pleasure boats, the main attraction here is the *Elizabeth II* (daily in summer, closed Mon. rest of the year; $3), a full-sized, square-rigged replica of the type of ship that carried colonists here from England 400-odd years ago.

Cape Hatteras National Seashore

The first piece of coastline to be protected as a national park, **Cape Hatteras National Seashore** stretches for 75 miles along the Atlantic Ocean. Starting in the north at Nags Head, and continuing south along slender Bodie, Hatteras, and Ocracoke Islands, the area preserved within Cape Hatteras National Seashore is the largest undeveloped section of coastline on the East Coast, providing an increasingly rare glimpse of nature amidst ever-encroaching development. The few old fishing villages that stood here when the seashore was set aside in the 1930s are unfortunately exempt from the anti-development prohibitions of the National Seashore; these have grown ugly and unwieldy. Nevertheless, the many miles in between remain almost entirely untouched.

For many visitors, the highlight of the National Seashore is the historic Cape Hatteras Lighthouse, a mile west of Hwy-12 at the south end of Hatteras Island. Others come here to enjoy the warm waters and strong, steady winds—two areas of Pamlico Sound on the inland side of Cape Hatteras have been set aside for windsurfers, dozens of whom

Warmed by the Gulf Stream currents, the Outer Banks beaches are some of the best in the world, but the waters do not warm up appreciably until south of Oregon Inlet, and swimming in the northern stretches remains quite invigorating until July.

The section of Pamlico Sound known as **Canadian Hole,** between the towns of Avon and Buxton, is rated as one of the best windsurfing spots on the East Coast.

Cape Hatteras Lighthouse, Cape Hatteras, N. C.

flock here on summer days to what's considered one of the finest sailboarding and kite-surfing spots in the United States. And of course, there are miles of open beaches, perfect for aimless strolling.

At the north end of Cape Hatteras, eight miles south of Nags Head, there's a National Seashore **visitors center** (daily; 252/473-2111) and a nature trail winding along Pamlico Sound at the foot of **Bodie Island Lighthouse,** the first of three historic towers along the Hatteras coast. On the ocean side of Hwy-12, **Coquina Beach** has a broad strand, lifeguards and showers in summer, and the remains of a wooden schooner that was wrecked here in the 1920s.

Continuing south, across the Oregon Inlet (where there's a first-come, first-served campground), Hwy-12 runs through the 6,000-acre **Pea Island National Wildlife Refuge,** which was established in 1938 to protect the nesting grounds of loggerhead sea turtles, as well as the coastal wetlands essential to the survival of the greater snow goose and other migratory waterfowl. South of the refuge, a few short barrages of vacation condos and roadside sprawl—go-cart parks, mini-golf courses, and a KOA Kampground—line the highway between Rodanthe and Salvo, before the road reaches the heart of the park, where high sand dunes rise along 15 miles of undeveloped oceanfront.

Avon and Buxton: Cape Hatteras Lighthouse

At the rough midpoint of Hatteras Island, the vacation town of **Avon** stretches for a couple of miles along Hwy-12 before the road hits the Canadian Hole windsurfing area, two miles south of town. After another few miles of natural dunes, the road bends sharply to the west; continuing south here brings you to the main **Cape Hatteras National Seashore visitors center** (daily in summer only; 252/995-4474) and the famous **Cape Hatteras Lighthouse.** At 208 feet, the black-and-white-striped lighthouse is the tallest brick lighthouse in the United States, visible from as far as 25 miles. However, because the ocean here

Hurricanes!

If you're traveling along the East Coast in late summer, be aware that the farther south you go the more likely you are to encounter one of Mother Nature's most powerful phenomena, the hurricane. All across the southeastern United States, hurricane season begins in June and lasts through November, and the threat of a storm can put a sudden end to the summer fun. Hurricanes are tropical storms covering upwards of 400 square miles, with winds reaching speeds of 75 to 150 mph or more. These storms form as far away as Africa, and sophisticated warning systems are in place to give coastal visitors plenty of time to get out of harm's way. Radio and TV stations broadcast storm watches and evacuation warnings, and if you hear one, heed it and head inland to higher ground.

Even more dangerous than the high winds of a hurricane is the storm surge—a dome of ocean water that can be 20 feet high at its peak, and 50 to 100 miles wide. Ninety percent of hurricane fatalities are attributable to the high waves of a storm surge, which can wash away entire beaches and intensify flooding in coastal rivers and bays many miles upstream from the shore. The strongest hurricane recorded in the United States was the Labor Day storm of 1935, which killed 500 people and destroyed the Florida Keys Railroad. More recent hurricanes include Hurricane Andrew in 1992, which killed 54 people and caused more than $25 billion worth of damage, and the multiple 'canes that pounded Florida in 2004. The levee breaks that flooded New Orleans made 2005's Hurricane Katrina by far the most costly U.S. hurricane, but the deadliest hurricane on record hit Galveston Island, Texas in 1900, killing more than 6,000 people—in human terms by far the worst natural disaster in United States history.

Blackbeard the Pirate

Wandering around the idyllic harbor of Ocracoke, it's hard to imagine that the waters offshore were once home to perhaps the most ferocious pirate who ever sailed the Seven Seas—Blackbeard. The archetypal pirate, even in his day, when piracy was common, Blackbeard was famous for his ruthlessness and violence as much as for his long black beard and exotic battle dress, wearing six pistols on twin gunbelts slung over his shoulders and slashing hapless opponents with a mighty cutlass. His pirate flag featured a heart dripping blood, and a skeleton toting an hourglass in one hand and a spear in the other.

For all his near-mythic status, Blackbeard's career as a pirate was fairly short. After serving as an English privateer in the Caribbean during Queen Anne's War, in 1713 Blackbeard (whose real name was Edward Teach) turned to piracy, learning his trade under the pirate Benjamin Hornigold. Outfitted with four stolen ships, 40 cannons, and a crew of 300 men, Blackbeard embarked on a reign of terror that took him up and down the Atlantic coast of the American colonies. After five years of thieving cargoes and torturing sailors, Blackbeard was confronted off Ocracoke by forces led by Lt. Robert Maynard of the Royal Navy, and during a ferocious battle on November 22, 1718, the pirate and most of his men were killed. Blackbeard himself was stabbed 25 times, and his head was sliced off and hung like a trophy on the bowsprit of his captor's ship.

Though there is no evidence that he ever buried any treasure anywhere near Ocracoke, Blackbeard's ship, the *Queen Anne's Revenge,* was discovered in 1996 off Bogue Bank, and some cannons and other objects recovered from the pirate's ship are being preserved by the North Carolina Maritime Museum in Beaufort. Blackbeard's legend, to be sure, lives on.

has been slowly eroding away the beach (when the lighthouse was built in 1870, it was a quarter mile from the waves; by 1995 the coast was a mere 120 feet away from its base), in 1999 the National Park Service succeeded in lifting the 3,000-ton lighthouse onto rails and shifting it a quarter mile inland. If you feel fit, climb the stairs (12 stories' worth, each way; $6) to the top of the lighthouse for a grand view—one that gives the clearest sense of just how narrow and transitive the Outer Banks really are.

The village of Frisco, five miles north of the Hatteras ferry terminal, holds the small but surprisingly good **Native American Museum** (closed Mon.; $5; 252/995-4440), which boasts an extensive collection of artifacts from several tribes, including those from the Cape Hatteras area, and Hopi and Navajo crafts.

Farther along, at the end of this road, there's a summer-only, first-come, first-served campground.

From the Cape Hatteras Lighthouse, Hwy-12 bends west and south through **Buxton** and **Frisco,** where you will find a gauntlet of motels, gas stations, and fast-food restaurants at the commercial center of Cape Hatteras. The very popular **Fish House** (252/995-5151) is on the main highway next to Cape Hatteras High School. Buxton's motels, like the **Lighthouse View** (252/995-5680 or 800/225-7651) or the **Croatoan Inn** (252/995-5968 or 800/635-6911), are reasonably priced (around $100 a night in summer) and clean. Ocean beaches here at the very tip of the cape are among the most spectacular anywhere; south-facing, they tend to pick up some of the most extreme surf—especially when hurricanes hit—which is why Buxton and Frisco are the local surfing capitals.

More restaurants and motels (including a Holiday Inn Express) await you in **Hatteras,** at the southern end of the island. From here, state-run **ferries** (5 AM–midnight; free) shuttle every half hour across to Ocracoke Island, another mostly unspoiled barrier island where you'll find great beaches and the pretty village of Ocracoke, at the island's southern tip.

Ocracoke

About the only Outer Banks town that hasn't lost its small-scale charm, **Ocracoke** is a great place to spend an afternoon or two, walking or cycling along unpaved back streets lined by overgrown gardens and weathered old homes. Since it's easy to reach from the mainland, via ferries from Swan Quarter and from Cedar Island, Ocracoke is a popular destination, but the

The carnivorous **Venus Flytrap,** which Charles Darwin called "the most wonderful plant in the world," does not grow wild in any part of the world except the seacoast Carolinas.

tourism here is so low-key it still feels like a place you can discover for yourself.

The ferries from the mainland south of Ocracoke drop you at the heart of town. Coming in from the north on Hwy-12, you pass through a short strip of real estate agencies and restaurants like **Howard's Pub** (252/928-4441), a local institution whose rooftop, ocean-view deck is a very pleasant place to eat fresh local seafood and sample one or more of its 200 different beers.

From Hwy-12, a number of small back roads (including oak-lined Howard Street, and another called simply "Back Road," which runs past **Teach's Hole,** a shop dedicated to the pirate Blackbeard) are worth exploring—especially by bike, the best way to get around Ocracoke. Just south of the harbor, Point Road runs west to the squat, whitewashed 1823 Ocracoke Lighthouse.

Ocracoke Practicalities

Ocracoke's small and photogenic harbor is ringed by low-key, low-rise restaurants, bike rental stands, hotels, bars, and B&Bs. Many of the restaurants ringing the Ocracoke harbor morph into bars after dark. All are friendly and in-formal, and most have some kind of live music during the summer season, making wandering around town a prime visitor activity. Away from the harbor, the **Back Porch** (252/928-6401) on Back Road is rated as one of the Outer Banks' best restaurants.

There are no chain hotels on Ocracoke (which may in itself be reason enough to visit!), and local places are generally down-to-earth, not fancy. The oldest lodging option is **Blackbeard's Lodge** ($80 and up; 252/928-3421), a rambling old motel on Back Road. Another characterful place is the 100-year-old **Island Inn** ($75 and up; 252/928-4351), near the harbor.

Right across from the ferry landing, there's a very helpful **visitors center** (252/928-4531) that has complete information on Ocracoke and the rest of Cape Hatteras. Running between Ocracoke on Cape Hatteras, and two places on the North Carolina mainland (Cedar Island and Swan Quarter), the state-run ferry departs approximately every two hours (every three hours in winter) and takes close to 2.5 hours each way.

The cost is about $15 per car; call 800/BY-FERRY for current schedules and further information.

From Cedar Island, it's close to an hour's drive along US-70 to the next big city, Beaufort.

Cape Lookout National Seashore

If you like the look of Cape Hatteras but want to avoid the crowds, plan a visit to the much wilder **Cape Lookout National Seashore,** another series of barrier islands, which stretch for 55 miles from Ocracoke to the south near Beaufort. It's accessible only by boat, and there are few roads or services once you're there, but it's a lovely place to hike or camp, collect seashells, or just wander along the peaceful shore, exploring the remains of cabins and abandoned villages. Day trips to Point Lookout leave from Beaufort on the "World's Largest Speedboat," the Lookout Express ($15; 252/728-6997), or you can usually arrange a charter from Ocracoke.

Beaufort and Morehead City

Known as Fishtown until it was renamed in 1722, the charming 18th-century town of **Beaufort** (pop. 3,800) has quiet streets lined with churches, cemeteries filled with weather-stained monuments, and whitewashed houses with narrow porches. The nautical-themed shops and restaurants along the water on busy Front Street, three blocks south of US-70, attract tourists and boaters traveling along the Intracoastal Waterway. The spacious **North Carolina Maritime Museum** (daily; free; 252/728-7317), at 315 Front Street, features many informative exhibits on the region's nautical and natural history, as well as a truly impressive display of over 1,000 beautiful seashells.

North Carolina's beaches are prime nesting grounds for endangered **loggerhead sea turtles.** These huge turtles come ashore mid-May to late August by the light of the full moon. Each female lays over 100 eggs, which hatch at the end of summer.

Not surprisingly, Beaufort, North Carolina is often confused with Beaufort, South Carolina. The former is pronounced BO-fort; the latter is pronounced BYOO-furd.

The museum also sponsors an annual Wooden Boat Show, held the last weekend in September.

Beaufort has one unique place to eat: **Clawson's** (252/728-2133), a burger and seafood place housed in an old grocery store at 425 Front Street, that's been in business since 1905. For even more famous burgers (and shrimp burgers!), head along to **El's Drive-In** (252/726-3002), on US-70 a mile south of the bridge to Atlantic Beach.

While Beaufort may be prettier, you'll find the best food in burly **Morehead City,** three miles west of Beaufort and across the bridge. Try the homemade seafood-cocktail sauce and Tarheel hush puppies at the **Sanitary Fish Market & Restaurant** (252/247-3111) at 501 Evans Street; it's easy to find amidst the sportfishing boats a block off US-70.

Bogue Bank: Fort Macon

More barrier island beach resorts line **Bogue Bank,** which runs south of Morehead City in a nearly east–west orientation for some 25 miles. The half dozen family-oriented resort towns have freely accessible—but quite often crowded—beaches. The largest, **Atlantic Beach,** across a bridge from Morehead City, has a boardwalk backed by a go-cart track and a small amusement arcade. The newly expanded **State Aquarium** (daily; $8), five miles west of town on Hwy-58, features extensive displays on the local loggerhead sea turtles.

At the northeast end of Bogue Bank stands **Fort Macon State Park** (daily; free), which centers on a massive pre–Civil War fortress overlooking the harbor entrance. The penta-gon-shaped masonry fort, com-

pleted in 1834, was captured early in the Civil War by the Confederacy. In April 1862, Union forces retook Fort Mason after a bombardment and controlled Beaufort for the rest of the war.

Camp Lejeune and Jacksonville

Midway between Beaufort and Wilmington, much of the coastline is taken over by the 100,000-acre U.S. Marine Corps base of **Camp Lejeune.** Established during World War

II and now home to the crack rapid deployment forces and an urban combat training center, Camp Lejeune is open to visitors interested in a nose-to-nose encounter with tanks, humvees, and other lethal machines. Sentries will check you in and out at both ends of the surprisingly scenic 25-mile drive across the base along Hwy-172, which serves as a shortcut to looping US-17.

At the northwest corner of Camp Lejeune, **Jacksonville** (pop. 66,715) is little more than a civilian adjunct to the base, with all the gas stations, fast-food franchises, and tattoo parlors Lejeune's 45,000 Marines and their dependents could want. One sobering sight is on the edge of town, just off Hwy-24 (opposite a Sonic Drive-In): the 50-foot-long granite wall of the **Beirut Memorial** remembers the more than 250 Camp Lejeune Marines killed in Beirut in 1983 by a suicide bomber. Alongside a list of their names are the words "They Came in Peace."

Surf City to Wrightsville Beach

South of Camp Lejeune, US-17 runs through the lushly forested lowlands around Holly Ridge, while Hwy-210 cuts across a series of narrow barrier islands. The waterfront is mostly private, backed by beach house after beach house (rentals aplenty, if you can manage to stay for a full week), but with a few parking areas for passing travelers. The clean strands and clear blue waters continue through sleepy Topsail Beach, home to the nation's only hospital for injured loggerhead turtles. The 20-odd "patients" are cared for by volunteers at 822 Carolina Boulevard downtown, across from the water tower.

Most of this stretch of coastline is dedicated to low-key, by-the-week family vacations, but the town of **Wrightsville Beach** has a bit more going on. Located 10 miles east of US-17 via US-74 or US-76, it's not all that different from dozens of other coastal vacation communities, but proximity to the lively city of Wilmington makes it a great place to stop. Places to stay along the beach include the comfortable **Blockade Runner Resort** ($99–300; 910/256-2251) at 275 Waynick Boulevard, which has a good restaurant, two bars, and bicycle, boat, and kayak rentals.

Wilmington

Though it's surrounded by the usual miles of highway sprawl, the downtown business district of **Wilmington** (pop. 75,838) is unusually attractive and well preserved, its many blocks of historic buildings stepping up from the Cape Fear River waterfront. The largest city on the North Carolina coast, Wilmington was of vital importance to the Confederate cause during the Civil War, when it was the only southern port able to continue exporting income-earning cotton, mostly to England, in the face of the Union blockade. Wilmington also played an important role before and during the Revolution, first as a center of colonial resistance, and later as headquarters for British Gen. Cornwallis.

In the book and movie *Gone With the Wind,* dashing southern hero Rhett Butler spent the Civil War as a Wilmington-based blockade runner, evading the U.S. Navy.

Transcontinental I-40 starts in Wilmington and runs west to Southern California. The first stretch is named in honor of local basketball superstar **Michael Jordan,** and another sign gives the road's western destination: "Barstow, Calif. 2,554 miles."

Despite its lengthy and involved military history, Wilmington itself has survived relatively unscathed and now possesses one of the country's more engaging small-town streetscapes. Cobblestone wharves and brick warehouses line the Cape Fear River, which also provides moorage for the massive 35,000-ton battleship USS *North Carolina* (daily; $12), across the river. A couple of the warehouses, like the Cotton Exchange at the north end, have been converted to house boutiques and restaurants. A block inland, Front Street is the lively heart of town, a franchise-free stretch of book and music stores, cafés, and other businesses that's often used by film crews attempting to re-create a typically American "Main Street" scene. Films like *Blue Velvet,* and TV's teenage soap opera *Dawson's Creek,* were shot at Wilmington's massive Screen Gems studio and in surrounding locales.

Thanks in large part to its significant TV and moviemaking business, Wilmington has a number of excellent places to eat, like the comfortable **Caffé Phoenix** (910/343-1395) at 9 S. Front Street, an excellent Italian bistro serving fresh pasta dishes

Wilmington waterfront

and pizzas. Within stumbling distance are bars like the rough-hewn **Barbary Coast,** 116 S. Front Street (910/762-8996). For a taste of top-quality traditional Southern food—grits with everything—try the **Dixie Grill,** 116 Market Street (910/762-7280), where you can work off the calories with a game of pool.

Rates at Wilmington's many chain motels and hotels are refreshingly low; try the riverfront **Hilton** ($99 and up; 910/763-5900).

South of Wilmington, US-17 runs inland, so if you want to stick close to the coast, take Hwy-179, which curves along the shore past the rambling towns of **Ocean Isle Beach** and **Sunset Beach** before rejoining US-17 at the South Carolina border.

Cape Fear

Though it has lent its name to two of the most terrifying movies ever made, **Cape Fear** is not at all a scary place—so long as you stay on land. The name was given to it by sailors who feared its shipwrecking shoals, and hundreds of vessels have indeed been wrecked off the cape, including dozens of Confederate blockade-runners sunk during the Civil War embargo of Wilmington harbor.

Between the east and west banks of the Cape Fear River, a **ferry** (800/BY-FERRY) runs about once an hour between Fort Fisher and Southport.

South of Wilmington, US-421 runs along the east bank of the Cape Fear River through typical barrier island beach resort towns like Carolina Beach and Kure Beach. Near the south end of the island, **Fort Fisher State Historic Site** features the earthwork fortification that enabled Wilmington harbor to remain open to ships throughout most of the Civil War. The fortress looks more like a series of primitive mounds than an elaborate military installation, but its simple sand piles proved more durable against Union artillery than the heavy masonry of Fort Sumter and other traditional fortresses. A **visitors center** (daily; free; 910/458-5538) describes the fort's role, with details of the war's heaviest sea battle, when Union ships bombarded Fort Fisher in January 1865. Surrounding lands have been left wild, and a nice outpost of the State Aquarium has tanks of local sealife.

On the west bank of the Cape Fear River, Hwy-133 winds up at the pleasure-craft harbor of **Southport,** which is the halfway point between New York City and Miami, attracting sailors traveling the Intracoastal Waterway. It's also the site of the large Brunswick nuclear power plant.

Cape Fear itself is formed by **Bald Head Island,** at the mouth of the Cape Fear River, reachable only by boat from Southport. The **Old Baldy Lighthouse** on the island is the state's oldest, built in 1817.

SOUTH CAROLINA

Just beyond the border into South Carolina, you suddenly hit the exuberant mega-tourism of the "Grand Strand," a 25-mile-long conglomeration of resort hotels, amusement arcades, and Coney Island–style Americana that centers on **Myrtle Beach,** the state's number-one tourist destination. South of here things quiet down considerably, as coastal US-17 winds past the lush lowland marshes, passing through historic **Georgetown** and numerous preserved plantations before reaching **Charleston,** one of the most gracious and engaging cities in the southern United States.

Myrtle Beach: The Grand Strand

Standing at the center of the Grand Strand, **Myrtle Beach** (pop. 32,000) is one of the largest and most popular beach resorts in the country, attracting some 13 million visitors every year. It's a huge place, with mile after mile of motels, Wal-Marts, and fast-food franchises lining all the main roads. Long famous for its golf courses (and for having the world's biggest collection of miniature golf courses), in recent years—its landmark Pavilion amusement park was demolished in 2006, to make room for yet another mall—Myrtle Beach has swapped roller coasters and beachfront fun for shopping and merchandising.

The spring- and summer-blooming crepe myrtle trees, with long branches of purple and red flowers, gave Myrtle Beach its name. The old beachfront Pavilion in Myrtle Beach was the 1950s birthplace of **"The Shag,"** a sexually explicit slow jitterbug that is now the official South Carolina state dance.

Myrtle Beach boasts more **golf courses,** including a bewildering array of miniature golf courses, than anywhere else in the country. Most have castaway or pirate themes; one's based upon the TV show *Gilligan's Island.*

Myrtle Beach Practicalities

If you don't mind keeping your tongue wedged firmly in your cheek, the

South of the Border

If the Grand Strand and Myrtle Beach haven't satisfied your need for roadside kitsch, or if you're bombing along I-95 looking for a place to take a break, head to South of the Border, the world's largest and most unapologetic tourist trap. Located just south of the North Carolina state line at I-95 exit 1, South of the Border is a crazy place with no real reason to exist, yet it draws many thousands of visitors every day to a 135-acre assembly of sombrero-shaped fast-food stands, giant video arcades, souvenir shops, and innumerable signs and statues of the South of the Border mascot, Pedro, including one that's nearly 100 feet tall.

Many roadside businesses suffered when a new Interstate or bypass left them high and dry, but in the case of South of the Border, the opposite is true. It started as a fireworks and hot dog stand along US-301 in the early 1950s, but when highway engineers decided to locate I-95 here, its middle-of-nowhere locale suddenly became prime highway frontage, and owner Alan Shafer (who died in 2001 at the age of 87) made playful use of its location (50 feet south of the state line) to create this pseudo-Mexican "South of the Border" village–cum–roadside rest stop. Though the complex itself is hard to miss, with its sombrero-clad concrete brontosaurus and 20-story Sombrero Tower giving a panoramic view of the Interstate, I-95 drivers from both directions get plenty of notice of their approach, thanks to the hundreds of garish billboards that line the road, saying silly things like "Chili Today, Hot Tamale," the subliminal messages all but forcing you to pull off and chow down on a taco or three and buy some mass-produced keepsake you'll throw away as soon as you get home.

South of the Border is open 24 hours every day, and, along with the myriad of tourist tack, it also has two gas stations and a pleasant, 300-room motel ($50 and up; 843/774-2411).

Myrtle Beach area can be fun, and it's definitely a mecca for fans of ersatz "themed" restaurants: Planet Hollywood, NASCAR Café, Hard Rock Cafe, Margaritaville, and Caddyshack all vie for attention in the massive Broadway-at-the-Beach complex on Kings Highway, north of US-501. Owned by the same company that tore down the Pavilion, this is the biggest attraction in Myrtle Beach, but despite the name, Broadway-at-the-Beach is over a mile from the ocean.

If you want a more genuine taste of Myrtle Beach, some of the best places to eat are in Murrells Inlet. One very nice "old-time" Myrtle Beach restaurant, the **Sea Captain's House** (843/448-8082) at 3000 N. Ocean Boulevard, has survived the developers' blitz and is still serving three delicious meals a day, just as it has since 1954. The seafood is great, and just about every table has an ocean view.

Murrells Inlet

There *may* be more picturesque places elsewhere in the state, but the as-yet-unspoiled fishing village of **Murrells Inlet,** 12 miles south of Myrtle Beach, is definitely worth a stop for the chance to sample the dozens of excellent seafood restaurants lining a short business loop off US-17. For the best and freshest seafood, head to **Nance's Shellfish** (843/651-2696), right on the water at 4883 US-17. Another good bet is **Flo's Place** (which has great key lime pie) at the north end of town at 3797 US-17 (843/651-7222). And if you've got the time and inclination to catch your own seafood, sportfishing charter boats run from the marina, or you can put on some waders and head into the waters in search of clams, mussels, oysters, and crabs.

Brookgreen Gardens and Huntington Beach State Park

One of the most popular and pleasant gardens in South Carolina, **Brookgreen Gardens** (daily; $12), 16 miles south of Myrtle Beach, is a non-profit, 4,000-acre park on the lushly landscaped grounds of four colonial-era indigo and rice plantations. Oak trees laden with Spanish moss stand alongside palmettos, dogwoods, and azaleas, as well as hundreds of sculptures, including many done by the owner, Anna Hyatt Huntington, who developed the site in the 1930s. Alligators and otters play in the simulated swamp and many species of birds fly around enclosed aviaries in a section of the gardens set aside as a wildlife park.

Across the highway is the 2,500-acre **Huntington Beach State Park** ($5 per car; 843/237-4440), which sits on land carved out of the Huntington estate that is leased to South Carolina. Besides a nice beach and a popular campground, it features the Moorish-style castle called Atalaya, Anna Huntington's studio.

> Carry insect repellent and be prepared for **mosquitoes,** especially late in the afternoon, almost everywhere along the muggy South Carolina coast.

Pawleys Island and Hobcaw Barony

South of the commercial chaos of Myrtle Beach, travelers in search of serene tranquility have long appreciated **Pawleys Island.** The rope hammocks for which the island is best known aptly symbolize this generally relaxed, weatherworn community, where a few traditional tin-roofed shacks mix with ever-increasing numbers of multi-million-dollar mock-antebellum mansions. It's mostly private, apart from the plush environs of **Litchfield Plantation** ($160 and up; 800/869-1410), a 600-acre resort on the grounds of a colonial-era plantation. The poet and novelist James Dickey, author of

Deliverance, liked it so much he lived here for his last 25 years and is buried in the small Pawleys Island cemetery.

An even more extensive and intimate (and affordable) taste of the old-fashioned Lowcountry life is available just down the road from Pawleys Island. Spreading along the north bank of the Pee Dee River, a mile north of Georgetown on US-17, **Hobcaw Barony** is a 17,500-acre estate that was once the winter home of 1920s financier and New Deal–era statesman Bernard Baruch and his daughter, Belle. The extensive, mostly undeveloped grounds are home to two university research centers specializing in coastal ecology, and the main homes and plantation buildings have been kept in original condition, complete with one of very few surviving slave streets. Along with preserving these historic quarters and the regional history they represent, the nonprofit educational foundation that runs Hobcaw Barony offers half-day tours to school groups and individuals (Tues.–Fri.; $20; 843/546-4623). Tours start at the **visitors center and museum** (Mon.–Fri.; free) along US-17.

One of the more unusual radio stations in the country, **WLGI 90.9 FM,** is operated by the Ba'hai faith and broadcasts a commercial-free mix of classic 1970s soul, contemporary jazz, and messages of peace, love, and understanding. To learn more, call 800/228-6483.

Georgetown

Site of a short-lived Spanish settlement in 1526, the first European outpost in North America, **Georgetown** later became the rice-growing center of colonial America. Bounded by the Sampit and Pee Dee Rivers and the narrow inlet of Winyah Bay, Georgetown is one of the state's few deepwater harbors and home to two huge steel and paper mills along US-17, but its downtown district along Front Street is compact and comfortable, with dozens of day-to-day businesses and a few cafés and art galleries filling the many old buildings.

Three blocks south of US-17, at the east end of Front Street, there's a pleasant waterfront promenade, where the clock-towered old town market now houses the **Rice Museum** (closed Sun.; $5). A series of dioramas traces South Carolina's little-known history as the world's main rice and indigo producer, a past often over-shadowed by the state's later tobacco and cotton trade. The rest of town holds many well-preserved colonial and ante-bellum houses, churches, and commercial buildings.

Another South Carolina musical connection: **Chubby Checker** (of "The Twist" fame) was born inland from Georgetown in Spring Gully, near the town of Andrews.

A couple of good places to eat in Georgetown include sea-food specialties at the **River Room,** 801 Front Street (843/527-4110), and the locals' favorite **Thomas Cafe** (843/546-7776), next to the Rice Museum at 703 Front Street. For more infor-mation, or to pick up a self-guided-tour map of town, contact the **Georgetown County Chamber of Commerce** (843/546-8436 or 800/777-7705), on the waterfront at 1001 Front Street.

Hampton Plantation and McClellanville

The Santee Delta region along US-17 between Georgetown and Charleston once held dozens of large and hugely profit-able plantations. One of the best preserved of these is now the **Hampton Plantation State Park,** located 15 miles south of Georgetown, then two miles west of US-17. Spreading out along the northern edge of Francis Marion National Forest, the 320-acre grounds feature a white wooden Greek Revival manor house (tours Thurs.–Mon. 1–4 PM; $4) that once wel-comed George Washington. The manor house was later home to Archibald Rutledge, poet laureate of South Carolina from 1934 until his death in 1973.

South from Hampton Plantation along US-17, a small sign marks the turn-off to the quaint Lowcountry fishing village of **McClellanville** (pop. 496). A short drive past moss-draped oak trees brings you to the town dock, where some of the last portions of South Carolina's shrimp and crab catch get un-loaded and shipped to market.

Cape Romain National Wildlife Refuge

Dense forests stretch west from the highway, while the un-spoiled **Cape Romain National Wildlife Refuge** stretches south of McClellanville nearly to Charleston, forming one of the largest and most important sanctuaries for migratory birds on the East Coast. Thousands of great blue herons, pelicans, terns, and ducks join the resident population of wild turkeys, feral pigs, deer, and alligators. To get a glimpse of the diverse life protected here, visit the **Sewee Visitor Center** (daily; free; 843/928-3368), on US-17 at Awendaw. Exhibits inside explain the natural and human history of the region, and trails outside lead to a boardwalk viewing area and an enclosure that's home to native red wolves.

Directly across from the refuge entrance on US-17, you can appreciate other aspects of the area's culture at the homey **SeeWee Cafe** (843/928-3609), a general store turned restaurant serving homemade specialties, including a fabulously rich she-crab soup (served with a shot of sherry on the side). The ambience is perfect—tin cans still fill the shelves, and local fishermen stop by to offer their catches—and the low prices and friendly people make it worth planning your trip around.

Fort Moultrie and Mount Pleasant

Sitting at the entrance to Charleston harbor, across from its better-known sibling, Fort Sumter, **Fort Moultrie** (daily; $3) overlooks the Atlantic with good views of passing ships and the city of Charleston. The location alone would make Moultrie well worth a visit, but most come because of its vital role in American military history. Originally built from palmetto logs during the Revolutionary War, and since rebuilt many times, the fort is a testament to the development of coastal defenses. Its well-preserved sections date from every major U.S. war between 1812 and World War II, when Fort Moultrie protected Charleston harbor from roving German U-boats. But the fort is most famous for its role in the events of April 1861, when Fort Moultrie touched off the Civil War by leading the bombardment of Fort Sumter.

Fort Moultrie is easy to reach. From Mount Pleasant, a suburban community on the north bank of the Cooper River, across from Charleston, turn south from US-17 onto Hwy-703 then follow signs along Middle Street to the fort.

Along with Fort Moultrie, **Mount Pleasant** itself is worth visiting for the many African sweetgrass basketmakers who set up shop along US-17. While the roadside is rapidly filling up with suburban tract-house "plantations," in the warmer months women sit and weave these intricate

African sweetgrass basket

baskets at their ramshackle stands. Like so many other Lowcountry traditions, sweetgrass weaving may soon be a lost art, as younger women are increasingly reluctant to take on this low-paid work; it can take four to five hours to weave a basket that may sell for less than $30.

Fort Sumter National Monument

Commanding an island at the mouth of Charleston Harbor, **Fort Sumter National Monument** marks the site of the first military engagement of the Civil War. On April 12, 1861, a month after Abraham Lincoln's inauguration and four months after South Carolina had seceded from the United States, Confederate guns bombarded the fort until the federal forces withdrew. The structure was badly damaged, but no one was killed and the fort was held by the Confederates for the next four years, by which time it had been almost

a Grumman E-1B Tracer on the deck of the USS *Yorktown*, at Patriot's Point

completely flattened. Partly restored, but still a powerful symbol of the destruction wrought by the War Between the States, Fort Sumter is a key stop on any tour of Civil War sites.

The only way to visit Fort Sumter is by tour boat ($16; 800/789-3678); they leave from the north side of Charleston Bay at Patriot's Point, just off US-17 at the foot of the soaring new cable-stayed bridge across the Cooper River. (Other boats to Fort Sumter dock at Liberty Square in downtown Charleston.) Patriot's Point is also the anchorage of the aircraft carrier USS *Yorktown* (daily; $15), centerpiece of an excellent floating maritime museum that also includes WW II–era fighter planes, a destroyer that took part in D-Day, a Coast Guard cutter, and a Cold War–era submarine.

Beaufort

The second-oldest town in South Carolina, **Beaufort** (pop. 12,950; BYOO-furd) is a well-preserved antebellum town stretching along a fine natural harbor. Established in 1710, Beaufort stands on the largest of some 75 islands near the Georgia border; the town is perhaps best known as the home

Charleston

The Charleston accent is famous throughout the South. The word "garden" here is characteristically pronounced "gyarden," and "car" is "kyar," while the long "a" of Charleston (usually pronounced "Chaaahrleston") is as distinctive as JFK's "HAAH-vahd."

Established in 1670 as the capital of South Carolina, **Charleston,** more than any other Deep South city, proudly maintains the aristocratic traditions established during the plantation era. Then the elite would flee the heat, humidity, and mosquitoes of their lowland fiefdoms and come here to cavort in ballrooms and theaters. Still ruled by old money, though no longer the state capital, Charleston is both pretentious and provincial; locals like to say that Charleston is the place where the Ashley and Cooper Rivers meet to form the Atlantic Ocean. Though there are clear divides between the haves and have-nots, Charleston is surprisingly cosmopolitan, accommodating a historic ethnic mix of French Huguenots, Catholic Acadians, and Afro-Caribbeans, who collectively introduced the wrought-iron balconies and brightly colored cottages that give the city much of its charm. George Gershwin's opera *Porgy and Bess,* for example, was inspired by life in Charleston's Creole ghetto, specifically Cabbage Row, now a tidy brick-paved alley off Church Street.

Having suffered through a devastating earthquake, two wars, and innumerable hurricanes, Charleston has rebuilt and restored itself many times, yet it remains one of the South's most beautiful cities. Impressive neoclassical buildings line the streets, especially in the older, upmarket sections of town south of Broad Street and along the waterfront Battery. Charleston's many small, lush gardens and parks make it ideal for aimless exploring on foot rather than by car. If you'd like a friendly, intelligent guide to show you around, contact Mr. Ed Grimball (843/762-0056).

Many of the mansions and churches are open to visitors, but it's the overall fabric of Charleston, rather than specific sites, that is most memorable. That said, the 1828

Greek Revival **Edmonston-Alston House** (daily; $8) at 21 E. Battery is definitely worth a look, as is the beautiful spire of **St. Michael's Episcopal Church** (daily; donations) at 78 Meeting Street, which was modeled on the London churches of Sir Christopher Wren. A quarter mile north, at Church and Market Streets, is the open-air **City Market,** known as the "Ellis Island of Black America," since over a third of all slaves arrived in the colonies here. Once the commercial center of Charleston, the market now houses a range of souvenir shops and touristy restaurants.

Charleston's annual arts-and-opera **Spoleto Festival USA** (843/722-2764) is held over two weeks in May and June.

Charleston Practicalities

Thanks to its considerable tourist trade, Charleston supports a number of excellent eateries at all price ranges. Great breakfasts (as well as lunch, dinner, and Sunday brunch) are available at the very popular **Hominy Grill** (843/937-0930) at 207 Rutledge Avenue. Around the City Market, choose from the very popular **Hyman's Seafood** (843/723-6000) at 215 Meeting Street, which has a variety of basic but good-value fresh fish entrées for around $10; expect a wait. More sedate and expensive dinner places nearby include the stylish **SNOB** (Slightly North of Broad) at 192 E. Bay Street (843/723-3424), and **Magnolia's,** 185 E. Bay Street (843/577-7771), serving inventive takes on Charleston's traditional Lowcountry food.

Like its restaurants, Charleston's accommodation options tend toward the luxurious and expensive. Of the dozens of old-fashioned but well-appointed B&Bs (all of which charge upward of $200 a night), the elegant **John Rutledge House** (843/723-7999 or 800/476-9741) at 116 Broad Street offers four-star comfort in a converted 1763 house. The romantic, Queen Anne–style **Two Meeting Street Inn** (843/723-7322) at 2 Meeting Street has been welcoming guests for over 50 years. Hotels in and around the historic district are similarly expensive, though you'll find a very handy **Days Inn** ($100 and up; 843/722-8411) downtown at 155 Meeting Street.

Outside the historic area a half mile south of US-17, the **Charleston Visitor Center** (daily; 843/853-8000) at 375 Meeting Street is a good first stop; pick up a **day pass** ($5) to ride the DASH shuttle buses that loop around town.

of the massive U.S. Marine Corps Recruit Depot at nearby Parris Island, where new Marines undergo their basic training (graduation ceremonies, held Fri., are open to the public). Dozens of colonial-era and antebellum homes line Beaufort's quiet Bay Street waterfront, but only two, the **Verdier House** and the Greek Revival **Elliott House,** a block apart on Bay Street, are open to visitors. Verdier House offers tours, while the Elliott House is open as an art gallery.

Beaufort is a very enjoyable place to wander around and explore, and it has at least one great place to eat: **Blackstone's** (843/524-4330), off the main street at 205 Scott Street, where fans of the shrimp and grits and corned beef hash include local writer Pat Conroy. Places to stay include the waterfront **Best Western Sea Island Inn,** 1015 Bay Street (843/524-4121 or 800/528-1234), and the state's only four-star B&B, the lovely **Rhett House** ($160 and up; 843/524-9030) at 1009 Craven Street, where the film of Conroy's *The Prince of Tides* was shot on location.

As recently as 1960, the population of South Carolina's Sea Islands was predominantly African American—10 to 1 on average. Now, with all the recent "plantation-style" vacation resorts, the proportions have effectively been reversed. As a last defense against the dark arts of developers, traditional African American **Gullah culture** is celebrated in summer festivals and tourism literature promoting the Gullah-Geechee Heritage Coast.

South to Savannah: Hilton Head

From Beaufort, the easiest way south is to follow Hwy-170 all the way to

Savannah, or to detour east onto I-95. Otherwise, a pleasant but potentially confusing series of two-lane roads run around Hilton Head Island across the lowlands toward Georgia.

Near the southern tip of South Carolina, **Hilton Head Island** is the largest ocean island between Florida and New Jersey. It was first settled in 1663, but only since the late 1950s, when a bridge to the mainland was completed, has it really been on the map. The deluxe, 500-room, 5,000-acre **Sea Pines Resort,** 32 Greenwood Drive ($250 and up; 888/807-6873), is an international destination, and upscale golf courses and plantation-style estates abound around the island's 30,000 acres, as do mini malls and all the trappings of suburban America. There's also a very popular, family-friendly **Disney resort,** 22 Harbourside Lane ($175 and up; 843/341-4100).

> Along the Savannah River, which marks the boundary between South Carolina and Georgia, **Eli Whitney** invented the cotton gin in 1793 at Mulberry Grove plantation.

The "success" of Hilton Head has caused developers to set their sights on the rest of the Lowcountry, as shown by the opening of the super-plush **Palmetto Bluff** resort ($500 and up; 843/706-6500) at nearby Bluffton, where each of 50 waterfront cottages is outfitted with plasma TVs and a Sub-Zero fridge for that quintessential Lowcountry experience.

GEORGIA

The marshes and barrier islands that line the Atlantic Ocean along the Georgia coast are among the lesser-known treasures of the eastern United States. Geographically, the coastline consists of mostly roadless and largely unconnected islands, which makes coastal driving nearly impossible; the nearest north–south routes, I-95 and the older US-17, run roughly 15 miles inland, and only a few roads head east to the Atlantic shore. The lack of access has kept development to a minimum and has

also been a boon to wildlife—well over half the coastline is protected within state and federal parks, preserves, and refuges.

The "you-can't-get-there-from-here" aspect can make it

more than a little frustrating for casual visitors, but if you have the time and inclination, it also makes the Georgia coast a wonderful place to explore. The two main car-friendly destinations along the Georgia coast are **Tybee Island** in the north, east of Savannah, and the beautiful and history-rich **Golden Isles,** east of Brunswick. Both are great places to visit, and they offer an appetizing taste of the 100 miles of isolated shoreline Georgia otherwise keeps to herself.

Bonaventure Cemetery

The drive east from Savannah to the Atlantic Ocean passes through picturesque fishing villages standing out from serene marshlands, where a maze of riverlets and creeks weaves through the tall green reeds, and fishing boats bob along the tidal waters as they head off to harvest shrimp and oysters.

Whether or not you got obsessed with *Midnight in the Garden of Good and Evil,* the book that put Savannah back on the map in the 1990s, you'll enjoy visiting Bonaventure Cemetery, which features prominently in the story. Located east of Savannah proper, north of US-80 via Mechanics Avenue and Bonaventure Road, it is simply one of the most evocative corners of this characterful part of the country, where majestic old trees draped in mossy strands stand over abundant azaleas and all manner of monuments and memorials. No less a figure than naturalist John Muir, who camped here for a while immediately after the Civil War, called it "one of the most impressive assemblages of animal and plant creatures I have ever met." Songwriter Johnny Mercer of "Moon River" fame is buried here, along with centuries' worth of Savannahans.

Fort Pulaski

East of Bonaventure Cemetery, **Fort Pulaski National Monument** (daily; $2; 912/786-5787) is a well-preserved stone-and-brick fortress completed in 1848 at a commanding site at the mouth of the Savannah River. Its prominent island site originally held colonial-era Fort Greene, which was demolished by a hurricane in 1804 and replaced by the architecturally impressive, pentagon-shaped bulwark that survives in its battered and breached state today, surrounded by a moat and many acres of grassy lawn. Beautiful and endlessly photogenic, besides the military history Fort Pulaski preserves abundant natural habitat for all sorts of splendid creatures: eagles, falcons, and songbirds fly about, while manatees and turtles cruise through the lazy waters.

Beginning in 1829, construction of Fort Pulaski, proclaimed "as strong as the Rocky Mountains," took 18 years, used 25 million bricks, and cost just over a million dollars. During the Civil War, its seven-foot-thick walls withstood bombardment by the Union forces' new rifled cannon for only 30 hours, prompting the fort's surrender in April 1862.

Savannah Beach: Tybee Island

Spreading lazily over the easternmost of many islands filling the delta at the mouth of the Savannah River, the town of **Tybee Island** (pop. 2,842) is a funky old family-oriented resort, with four blocks of burger-and-corn-dog stands, taverns, amusement arcades, thrill rides, and miniature golf courses at the eastern end of US-80, just 18 miles east of central Savannah. Originally known as Savannah Beach, and locally famous for the annual Beach Bum's Parade before Labor Day, Tybee Island's main attraction is its endless, and usually uncrowded, powdery white-sand beaches, which spread to either side of the new pier and pavilion at the end of 16th Avenue.

At the north end of Tybee Island, from whence the Union forces bombarded Fort Pulaski during the Civil War, a centuries-old lighthouse stands next to the WW II–era concrete bunkers that house the **Tybee Museum** (daily; $4; 912/786-5801), which includes the old lighthouse keeper's cottage among its collections tracing the island's history.

Other draws here are the wacky, slightly ersatz, diner-style **Breakfast Club** (912/786-5984), right at the center of things at 1500 Butler Avenue, open daily for breakfast or an early lunch; if the line is too long, pop across the road to the **Sunrise** (912/786-7473).

Tybee Island's stretch of US-80 was home to the world's first **Days Inn** motel, but inexpensive accommodations can be hard to find. For a characterful, memorable stay, try the 100-year-old **Tybee Island Inn,** set in lovely gardens at the north end of

Savannah

Named the Most Beautiful City in North America by the style-arbiting Parisian newspaper *Le Monde,* **Savannah** (pop. 130,000) is a real jewel of a place. Founded in 1733 as the first settlement in Georgia, the 13th and final American colony, Savannah today preserves its original neoclassical, colonial, and antebellum self in a welcoming, unself-conscious way. Famous for having been spared by General Sherman on his destructive March to the Sea at the end of the Civil War, it was here that Sherman made his offering of "40 acres and a mule" to all freed slaves.

Before and after the war, Savannah was Georgia's main port, rivaling Charleston, South Carolina, for the enormously lucrative cotton trade, but as commercial shipping tailed off, the harbor became increasingly recreational—the yachting competitions of the 1996 Olympics were held offshore. Savannah, home of writer Flannery O'Connor and songsmith Johnny Mercer, also served as backdrop to the best-selling book *Midnight in the Garden of Good and Evil,* and numerous movies, most famously *Forrest Gump,* but it has resisted urges to turn itself into an "Old South" theme park; you'll have to search hard to find souvenir shops or overpriced knickknack galleries.

At the center of Savannah, midway down Bull Street between the waterfront and spacious Forsyth Park, **Chippewa Square** was the site of Forrest Gump's bus bench (the movie prop was moved to the visitors center and may one day be erected in bronze). **Reynolds Square,** near the waterfront, has a statue of John Wesley, who lived in Savannah in 1736–1737 and established the world's first Sunday School here. **Wright Square** holds a monument to Chief Tomochichi, the Native American tribal leader who allowed Oglethorpe to settle here, and **Forsyth Park,** at the south edge of the historic center, is modeled after the Place de la Concorde in Paris, surrounded by richly scented magnolias.

Forsyth Park

Another great place to wander is **Factor's Walk,** a promontory along the

Cotton Exchange

Savannah River named for the "factors" who controlled Savannah's cotton trade. This area holds the Cotton Exchange and other historic buildings, many of them constructed from 18th-century ballast stones. Linked from the top of the bluffs by a network of steep stone stairways and cast-iron walkways, **River Street** is lined by restaurants, and at the east end there's a statue of a girl waving; it was erected in memory of Florence Martus, who for 50 years around the turn of the 20th century greeted every ship entering Savannah harbor in the vain hope that her boyfriend would be on board.

March is when things get crazy here in Savannah: Thousands of visitors come to the bars along Congress Street for what has grown into the world's second-largest **St. Patrick's Day** celebration—only New York City's is bigger.

One of Savannah's more unusual tourist attractions is the **Juliet Gordon Low Birthplace,** at 142 Bull Street, a circa-1820 house that was the childhood home of the woman who introduced Girl Scouts to America in 1912. Current Girl Scouts gain a merit badge just by walking in the door.

Savannah Practicalities

Getting around is blissfully easy: Savannah is the country's preeminent walkers' town, with a wealth of historic architecture and

continued on next page

Savannah (continued)

a checkerboard of 22 small squares shaded with centuries-old live oak trees draped with tendrils of Spanish moss, all packed together in a single square mile. Savannah's sensible and very attractive modified grid plan makes finding your way so simple that it's almost fun to try to get lost.

For an unforgettable midday meal, be sure to stop at **Mrs. Wilkes' Dining Room** (Mon.–Fri. 11 A.M.–2 P.M.; 912/232-5997) at 107 W. Jones Street, a central Savannah home and former boardinghouse that still offers up traditional family-style Southern cooking—varying from fried chicken to crab stews, with side dishes like okra gumbo; sweet potato pie; red, green, or brown rice; and cornbread muffins. It's worth a trip from anywhere in the state—don't leave Savannah without eating here. On the south side of town on old US-80 at 1651 E. Victory Drive, **Johnny Harris** (912/354-7810) is Savannah's oldest restaurant and one of the fanciest fried chicken and barbecue places in the world.

Road-food fans may want to head a half mile south of downtown to the **Streamliner Diner,** at 102 W. Henry Street, a gorgeously restored 1938 Worcester diner operated by (and across the street from) the Savannah College of Art & Design (SCAD), which has taken over many of the city's older buildings and converted them into art studios, galleries, and cafés.

Places to stay in Savannah vary from quaint B&B inns to stale high-rise hotels. For the total Savannah experience, try the **Bed and Breakfast Inn** ($150 and up; 912/238-0518) at 117 W. Gordon Street, which has very nice rooms in an 1853 townhouse off Monterey Square. At the **River Street Inn** ($150 and up; 912/234-6400 or 800/253-4229), at 115 E. Bay Street, well-appointed rooms fill a converted antebellum cotton warehouse, right on Factor's Walk at the heart of the Savannah riverfront. Nearby at 201 W. Bay Street, the large **Inn at Ellis Square** ($125 and up; 912/236-4440 or 800/325-2525) has standard hotel rooms (in a former Days Inn), right across from Factor's Walk.

The **Savannah Visitors Center** (912/944-0455), at 301 Martin Luther King Boulevard in the old Georgia Central railroad terminal just west of the historic center, has free maps and brochures and other information on the city.

the island, on the grounds of historic Fort Screven ($150 and up; 912/786-9255).

US-17: Midway

The section of US-17 south of the Ogeechee River, off I-95 between exits 14 and 12, offers shunpikers a 24-mile taste of old-style Lowland Georgia. Sometimes called the Old Atlantic Highway, it is a textbook example of how traveling the two-lane highways is superior in almost every way to hustling down the Interstates.

Along US-17, a small sign on the east side of the highway (a mile south of I-95 exit 67) welcomes travelers to the **Smallest Church in America,** a 12-seat cabin that's open 24 hours. Turn the lights out when you leave.

Midway along, the coincidentally named town of **Midway** (pop. 1,100) was founded back in 1754 by a band of New England colonists, two of whom (Lyman Hall and Button Guinett) went on to sign the Declaration of Independence as Georgia's self-declared representatives to the Continental Congress. The centerpiece of Midway, then and now, is 200-year-old **Midway Church,** which preserves the original pulpit and slave gallery; keys for the church are available at the adjacent **Midway Museum** (closed Mon.; $3; 912/884-5837).

Though redolent with ghosts of Georgia's past, Midway is still a living, breathing little place, with a great 1930s-era road-food restaurant, **Ida Mae & Joe's** (912/884-3388), serving up plates of fresh-fried catfish, chicken fingers, and fresh-made pies at 817 N. US-17.

Sapelo Island and Darien

For an unforgettable taste of the *real* pre–tourist industry Georgia coast, make your way east to **Sapelo Island,** which stretches offshore between Midway and Darien. The island is a stark, sparsely populated, mostly undeveloped, and generally fascinating place to spend some time, a truly wild landscape where alligators and ferocious feral pigs live free among remnants of colonial-era plantation agriculture and native Creek Indian shell middens dating back 6,000 years. Once a cotton plantation, worked by slaves whose 70-odd descendents live in Hog Hammock, Sapelo's only permanent community, the island is now owned by the state of Georgia and used as a marine biology research center.

A compelling nonfiction account of 1970s Darien, Melissa Fay Greene's ***Praying for Sheetrock*** describes how locals and legal activists used federal lawsuits to overcome the corrupt regimes of local government and law enforcement officials.

The Class A **Savannah Sand Gnats** (912/351-9150), a New York Mets farm club, play at WPA-built Grayson Stadium, off US-80 on the south side of town.

There is no real commercial development on Sapelo Island—no stores and no restaurants, so bring your own food and drink—just miles of beaches, marshlands, and open sea. Get there from the mainland hamlet of **Meridian,** where you can catch the state-run ferry for a four-hour guided tour (reservations required; adults $10, under 18 $6; 912/437-3224), which gives a full introduction to Sapelo Island life. For an even more memorable experience, arrange to stay overnight at **The Wallow** (912/485-2206), a small Hog Hammock B&B run by lifelong Sapelo Island resident Cornelia Bailey. There's a communal kitchen, or meals can be arranged in advance.

South of Sapelo Island near the mouth of the Altamaha River, which formed the rough and frequently fought-over boundary between British and Spanish parts of the New World, **Darien** (pop. 1,800) looks a lot like most other coastal Deep South towns, but it boasts a history to match many bigger or more famous destinations. After a small, 16th-century Spanish mission near here was destroyed by Native Americans, Darien was founded in 1736 by Scottish colonists (many named McIntosh, now the name of the surrounding county) near Fort King George, the first British outpost in what became Georgia. Darien later became a center of the lucrative early-19th-century rice trade, surrounded by plantations where the abuse of slaves inspired British actress Fanny Kemble's book-length indictment, *Journal of a Residence on a Georgia Plantation in 1838–39,* an influential abolitionist text.

Despite the many claims it could make to importance, Darien preserves its past in a matter-of-fact manner. The main attraction is the reconstructed **Fort King George,** a state historic site, a mile east of US-17 on Fort King George Drive (closed Mon.; $5).

Another intriguing place to visit is the **Hofwyl-Broadfield Plantation** (Thurs.–Sat.; $5), five miles south of Darien along US-17, where a well-preserved plantation home is surrounded by 1,200 acres of one-time rice fields that have reverted to cypress swamps. Displays inside the visitors center tell the story of how slaves were forced to labor in the sweltering, mosquito-plagued summer heat, building levees and doing the back-breaking work of planting, growing, and harvesting the rice.

Brunswick: The Golden Isles

Along the southeast Georgia coast, a patchwork of islands known as the Golden Isles offer a wide range of images and experiences. The largest and best known, **St. Simon's Island** is a mini Hilton Head, with many vacation resorts and a sizable year-round community. The center of activity on St. Simon's is at the south tip of the island, where the "village" consists of a central plaza and a few blocks of shops, saloons, and restaurants along Mallory Street, which leads down to the waterfront pier and a circa-1872 lighthouse. Sea kayaks, bicycles, and boats can be rented here, and there are a number of reasonable motels. For a carbo-loading breakfast or lunch, try the popular **Fourth of May Café** (912/638-5444), Ocean Boulevard at 321 Mallory.

The one real "sight" on St. Simon's Island is the **Fort Frederica National Monument,** at the northwest edge of the island, which protects the remains of the village surrounding what was once the largest fortress in the British colonies. Built in 1736 and abandoned in 1763, Fort Frederica played a vital role in keeping Georgia British, rather than Spanish; in 1742, a key battle was fought six miles south of the fort, at a site known as "Bloody Marsh."

For the total Golden Isles experience, splurge on a night or two at one of the country's plushest resorts, the four-star **Cloister Hotel** ($750 and up; 912/638-3611 or 800/SEAISLAND), which covers adjacent Sea Island with 36 holes of golf courses and 264 Spanish-style rooms. Presidents from Coolidge to Bush have vacationed here, the late JFK Jr. got married here, and the G8 economic summit has been held here, too, which should give you some idea of the elite character of the place.

Back on the mainland, heavily industrialized **Brunswick** (pop. 16,500) feels about as far from the genteel pleasures of the Golden Isles as you can be. Most vacationers pass through quickly on their way to and from the Golden Isles, but there is one great place to stop: the **Georgia Pig** (912/264-6664), southwest of town at the US-17 junction, just east of I-95 exit 29. Tucked away next to a gas station in a scruffy woodland, it looks like it's been there forever; the bare-bones decor—log rafters, pine picnic tables, and creaking front door—disappears when you bite into the juicy ribs and fabulous pulled-pork sandwiches, which are smoked in a hickory-fired oven right behind the counter.

Jekyll Island

Southeast of Brunswick, and developed in the late 1880s as a private, members-only resort for New York multimillionaires, **Jekyll Island** now offers a chance for those *not* in control of a Fortune 500 company to enjoy a generous slice of Golden Isles life. Now owned by the state of Georgia, a grand hotel and dozens of palatial vacation "cottages" that would look equally at home in Newport, Rhode Island, are accessible to the general public after a long life spent catering to the richest of the rich.

At the center of the island, and the best place to start a

visit, is the landmark **Jekyll Island Club Hotel** ($229 and up; 912/635-2600 or 800/535-9547). The very pleasant rooms here aren't *all* that expensive, considering the luxury you're swaddled in, and the setting is superb. Majestic oak trees dangling garlands of Spanish moss cover the 200-acre grounds, and within a short walk, many of the grand old mansions are now open for guided tours ($10). The nearby stables have been converted into a nice little **museum** (daily; free), which tells the whole Jekyll Island story.

Around the turn of the 20th century, the 50-odd members of the **Jekyll Island Club,** which included such names as Rockefeller, Carnegie, Morgan, and Vanderbilt, controlled as much as 20 percent of the world's wealth.

One new development here has been the **Georgia Sea Turtle Center** ($6; 912/635-4444), housed in the old Jekyll Island power plant at 214 Stable Road. This is one of the prime places for the study and rehabilitation of these lyrical swimmers, whose native habitats have been threatened by all the housing and resort development along the Atlantic shore.

Less than a mile east, the Atlantic oceanfront is lined by Beachview Drive and a five-mile-long beach—with the least developed stretches at the north and south ends of the island. Bike rentals—which really provide the best way to see the island—are available along Beachview Drive ($5/hr; 912/635-9801).

Cumberland Island National Seashore

Right on the Florida border, and once the private reserve of the Carnegie family, the **Cumberland Island National Seashore** is a 99-percent-uninhabited barrier island with miles of hiking trails and primitive backcountry camping along beaches and in palmetto forests. Also here is the unique **Greyfield Inn** (904/261-6408), the Carnegie family mansion now operated (by Carnegie heirs) as an unpretentious 16-room historic lodge that runs around $400 a night for two people, including gourmet meals and transportation from the mainland. (Bring your own bug spray!)

Unless you're a guest at the Greyfield, Cumberland Island is only accessible by a twice-daily ferry ($12 round-trip) from the town of St. Marys, 10 miles east of

St. Marys, Georgia, the main access to Cumberland Island, is also home to a huge U.S. Navy Base, home port of the nuclear-powered and -armed submarine fleet.

I-95 exit 1. For further details, contact the Cumberland Island National Seashore information and reservations center at 912/882-4336.

FLORIDA

Stretching some 600 miles between the Georgia border and Key West at its far southern tip, Florida offers something for everyone, from unsullied nature to the tackiest tourist traps in the land, and everything imaginable in between. More than anywhere else in the United States, the Florida landscape has been designed for tourists, and no matter what your fancy or fantasy, you can live it here, under the semitropical sun. The many millions who visit Disney World or flock to fashionable Miami Beach each year are doing exactly what people have come to Florida to do for over a century—enjoy themselves.

In the 1930s, when car travel and Florida tourism were both reaching an early peak of popularity, the roadside landscape was, in the words of the WPA *Guide to Florida,* lined by

Two men who made millions in the automobile industry have had immeasurable influence over the evolution of the Florida coast. Standard Oil baron **Henry Flagler** constructed the first railroad and built a chain of deluxe resort hotels from St. Augustine to Miami, while **Carl Fisher,** the developer of car headlights, promoted Florida's "Route 66," the Dixie Highway, and later helped to found Miami Beach. Their names reappear frequently wherever you travel along the Atlantic coast.

Of all the American colonies, only Florida remained loyal to the British crown during the Revolutionary War. After the war, the British ceded Florida to Spain, which eventually swapped it to the United States in 1821 in exchange for $5 million in assumed debt.

. . . signs that turn like windmills; startling signs that resemble crashed airplanes; signs with glass lettering which blaze forth at night when automobile headlights strike them; flashing neon signs; signs painted with professional touch; signs crudely lettered and misspelled. They advertise hotels, tourist cabins, fishing camps, and eating places. They extol the virtues of ice creams, shoe creams, cold creams; proclaim the advantages of new cars and used cars; tell of 24-hour towing and ambulance service, Georgia pecans, Florida fruit and fruit

juices, honey, soft drinks, and furniture. They urge the traveler to take designated tours, to visit certain cities, to stop at certain points he must see.

Despite the modern gloss of golf course estates and sprawling retirement communities, which tend to overshadow the substantial stretches of wide open beaches and coastal forest, Florida has a lengthy and fascinating history, with significant native cultures and, in **St. Augustine,** some of the oldest signs of European presence in North America, including the legendary Fountain of Youth. At the other end of the state, on the fringes of the Caribbean, **Key West** is a tropical paradise, founded by pirates four centuries ago and still one of the most lively and anarchic places in the United States. In between, our road-trip route passes through such diverse places as **Daytona Beach,** mecca for race car fans and a magnet for college kids on spring break; the launch pads and mission control centers of the **Kennedy Space Center;** the multicultural melting pots of **Miami** and **Miami Beach;** and, of course, the "Happiest Place on Earth," **Disney World.**

There are three main routes running north–south along

Florida's Atlantic coastline, and your travels will likely make use of at least a little of each one. The fastest route is the **I-95** freeway, which races uneventfully along, linking the major cities. The most scenic route is **Hwy-A1A,** a mostly two-lane highway that runs as close as possible to the shoreline, linking many gorgeous beaches but, because of the very flat topography and the extensive beachfront development, only rare glimpses of the open ocean. In between I-95 and Hwy-A1A runs historic **US-1,** part of the old Dixie Highway, which is lined by reminders of Florida's rich roadside heritage but which also passes through some of the state's less salubrious corners, especially in and around the larger cities. Our suggested route primarily follows coastal Hwy-A1A, but directions from other, faster routes are also given, so you can alternate freely and easily among them all.

Amelia Island

Entering Florida from Georgia across the St. Marys River, which flows east out of the Okefenokee Swamp to the Atlantic Ocean, you may want to skirt around the metropolitan sprawl of Jacksonville by following old US-17, or getting off I-95 at exit 129, to Hwy-A1A, which runs due east to the brilliant white-sand beaches and picturesque historic buildings of **Amelia Island.** The main community on the island is **Fernandina Beach** (pop 10,549), once the main port in northeast Florida. The eastern terminus of the first trans-Florida railroad, and long a popular tourist destination, Fernandina Beach retains many late-Victorian buildings, collected together in a wanderable 30-block historic district along the Amelia Island bayfront.

A local landmark, the **Florida House Inn** ($150 and up; 904/261-3300) at 22 S. 3rd Street is Florida's oldest hotel, welcoming travelers since 1857, while at the center of town the lively **Palace Saloon** (904/491-3332), at 117 Centre Street, is

FLORIDA HOUSE INN

another of "Florida's Oldest," with a lovely carved wood bar, very good burgers, and regular live reggae and other warm-weather music.

More history has been preserved at the north end of Amelia Island, adjacent to Fernandina Beach, where the well-preserved remnants of a pre–Civil War brick fortress stand in **Fort Clinch State Park** (daily; $6 per car; 904/277-7274), with 250 acres of marshes, sand dunes, and coastal hammock forests, plus a nice campground, along the edge of Cumberland Sound.

South of Fernandina Beach, Hwy-A1A follows Fletcher Avenue along Amelia Island's gorgeous white beaches, passing upscale resorts (including a Ritz-Carlton) before crossing over a bridge onto Talbot Island. Four miles south of the bridge, there's a turnoff west to the 3,000-acre **Kingsley Plantation** (daily; free; 904/251-3537), the last remaining antebellum plantation in Florida, where you can explore the elegant old lodge and remains of more than 20 slave cabins.

Continuing south, Hwy-A1A winds across the dense native jungles of **Little Talbot Island,** where a large **state park** (daily dawn–dusk; $5 per car; 904/251-2320) has hiking and cycling trails, a nice campground, and a magnificent beach. The scenic road, which has been dubbed the "Buccaneer Trail," eventually ends up at the terminal for the ferry to Mayport (every 30 min.; no RVs) across the St. Johns River.

Jacksonville Beach

East of Jacksonville, at the mouth of the St. Johns River, Hwy-A1A curves around a large U.S. Navy base (3rd largest in the U.S., specializing in helicopters, which

> Jacksonville, which covers over 840 square miles, is the largest city by area in the continental United States.

you'll often see hovering overhead), past the busy Bath Iron Works shipyard and the sizable fishing port of **Mayport,** where you can enjoy a quick bite at seafood shack **Singleton's,** (904/246-4442) 100 yards west of the ferry landing. From Mayport, Hwy-A1A zig-zags inland south and east, reaching the water again at **Jacksonville Beach,** a welcoming, family-oriented community with the usual gauntlet of cafés, mini-golf courses, and video arcades, and a nice beachfront centering on a small pier.

South of Jacksonville Beach spreads the enclave of **Ponte Vedra Beach,** where country club resorts replace roadside sprawl. Hwy-A1A bends inland through here, so if you want

Henry Flagler: Father of Florida Tourism

Though you've probably never heard of the man, you can't travel very far along the east coast of Florida without coming under the influence of Henry Flagler, who almost singlehandedly turned what had been swampy coastline into one of the world's most popular tourist destinations. After making a fortune as John D. Rockefeller's partner in the Standard Oil Company, in the early 1880s Flagler came to St. Augustine with his wife, who was suffering from health problems. He found the climate agreeable, but the facilities sorely lacking, so he embarked on construction of the 540-room Hotel Ponce de León, which opened in 1888. The hotel, the first major resort in Florida, was an instant success, and Flagler quickly expanded his operations, building the first railroad along the coast south to Palm Beach, where he opened the world's largest hotel, the now-demolished Royal Poinciana, in 1894, joined by The Breakers in 1901, and his own palatial home, Whitehall, in 1902.

Meanwhile, Flagler was busy extending his railroad south, effectively founding the new city of Miami in 1897 when he opened the deluxe Royal Palm Hotel. From Miami, he decided to extend his Florida East Coast Railway all the way to Key West, which at the time was Florida's most populous city, and the American deep-water port closest to the proposed Panama Canal. At a cost of $50 million and hundreds of lives, this amazing railroad was completed in 1912, but it lasted only two decades before a hurricane destroyed the tracks in 1935. The remnants of Flagler's railroad were used as the foundation for today's Overseas Highway, US-1, but Flagler himself never lived to see it: In 1913, a year after his railroad reached Key West, Henry Flagler fell down a flight of stairs and died at age 84.

to keep close to the shore (most of which is private), follow Hwy-203 instead, rejoining Hwy-A1A on the edge of town.

South of Ponte Vedra, Hwy-A1A passes a pair of beachfront state parks (the marvelous 12,000-acre **Guana River** and smaller **South Ponte Vedra**), both of which give access to usually uncrowded sands.

Fountain of Youth

North of St. Augustine, Hwy-A1A cuts inland from the shore, crossing a bridge over the North River, then following San Marco Avenue south into the center of St. Augustine past the Fountain of Youth. That's right, the Fountain of Youth. Though its efficacy has never been proven in court, there is an actual site where Spanish explorer Ponce de León, searching for a fabled spring that would keep him forever young, came ashore in 1513. Now a pleasant 20-acre park, facing Matanzas Bay about a mile north of central St. Augustine, the **Fountain of Youth** (daily 9 AM–5 PM; $8; 800/356-8222) preserves a naturally sulfurous spring (which you can drink from using Dixie cups—though there are no guarantees of immortality!), a burial ground, and remnants of a native Timucuan village and an early Spanish settlement.

St. Augustine

If you like history, architecture, sandy beaches, bizarre tourist attractions—or any combination of the above—you'll want to spend some time in St. Augustine. The oldest permanent settlement in the United States—though Santa Fe, New Mexico, makes a strong counterclaim to this title—**St. Augustine** was founded in 1565, half a century after Ponce de León first set foot here in 1513, looking for the Fountain of Youth. Under Spanish control, the town's early history was pretty lively, with Sir Francis Drake leveling the place in 1586.

Across the street from the Ripley's Believe It or Not!, a coquina stone ball known as the **Zero Milepost** marks the eastern end of the **Old Spanish Trail,** one of the earliest transcontinental highways. Marked and promoted from here west to San Diego, the Old Spanish Trail, like the Lincoln Highway and the Dixie Highway, preceded the system of numbered highways (Route 66 et al.), and provided a popular cross-country link.

The British, after trading Cuba for Florida at the end of the Seven Years' War, took control in 1763 and held St. Augustine throughout the American Revolution—during which Florida was staunchly loyal to King George. It served for many years as capital of Florida under both the British and Spanish, but after the Americans took over, the city lost that status to Tallahassee. St. Augustine subsequently missed out on much of Florida's 20th-century growth and development, which has allowed the preservation of its substantial historical remnants.

The heart of St. Augustine is contained within a walkably small area, centered on the Plaza de la Constitución, which faces east onto Matanzas Bay. Pedestrianized St. George Street runs north and south from here through the heart of historic St. Augustine, while two blocks west stands the city's most prominent landmarks: two grand, early 1900s hotels—the **Ponce de Leon** and the **Alcazar.** They were originally owned and operated as part of Henry Flagler's Florida empire but now respectively house **Flagler College** and the decorative arts collections of the **Lightner Museum** (daily; $10). Both are full of finely crafted interior spaces and well worth a look.

Though it's the compact size and overall historic sheen of St. Augustine that make it such a captivating place to spend some time, there are lots of individual attractions hawking themselves as important "historic sites," usually the oldest this-or-that in Florida, or even in the whole United States. The oldest **Wooden Schoolhouse,** at 14 St. George Street in the heart of historic St. Augustine, dates from 1750 and now features a push-button wax dummy of a schoolteacher, while the oldest **Store,** a block south of the main plaza at 4 Artillery Lane, has 100,000 items, all of them well past their turn-of-the-20th-century sell-by date. At the north end of St. George Street, an original city gate leads across San

Marco Avenue (Hwy-A1A) to another must-see tourist trap: the original **Ripley's Believe It or Not!** museum (daily; $12.95; 904/824-1606), an elaborate Spanish Revival mansion filled since 1950 with Robert Ripley's personal collection of oddities. Outside, in the parking lot, is a four-room "tree house," carved out of a California redwood tree in 1957.

These are fun in a tongue-in-cheek way, but the most impressive historic site is the remarkable **Castillo de San Marcos** (daily; $5), which dominates the St. Augustine waterfront. Built by Spain between 1672 and 1695, the Castillo saw its first battle in 1702, when British forces laid siege for 50 days but were unable to capture it, though they did once again level the adjacent town of St. Augustine. The Castillo was later used by the British to house American POWs during the Revolutionary War, and by the United States to house Native American prisoners captured during the Seminole War of 1835–1842 as well as during the later Indian Wars of the Wild West. Since 1924 it's been a National Monument and is open for walks along the ramparts, and for frequent ranger-guided tours.

One of many attractive things about St. Augustine is the almost total lack of franchised fast-food restaurants, at least in the historic downtown area. Instead, you can choose from all sorts of local places, like the **Florida Cracker Cafe** (904/829-0397) at 81 St. George Street, a casual seafood grill where you can sample the local delicacy, alligator tail. For fish-and-chips, try the **Milltop Tavern,** at the north end of St. George Street, which boasts good live music and a block-long bar. (Yes, it's a short block.) Another fun place to while away an evening is **Scarlett O'Hara's,** offering beers, burgers, and live music a block from Flagler College at 70 Hypolita Street.

Away from the historic core, heading south toward St. Augustine Beach, Hwy-A1A passes a series of roadside restaurants: the **Gypsy Cab Company,** 828 Anastasia (904/824-8244), is urbane. Fun and fairly good value, on St. Augustine Beach itself, **Po-Mar's,** at 6896 Hwy-A1A (904/471-0075) is a very popular sandwich and beer stand.

Unfortunately for present-day visitors, the grand old Ponce de Léon Hotel no longer welcomes overnight guests, but contemporary St. Augustine does offer a wide variety of accommodations, including the only B&B on Florida's Atlantic beachfront, the imaginatively named **Beachfront B&B** ($129 and up; 904/461-8727) at 1 F Street in St. Augustine Beach, where you can spend the night in one of six tastefully decorated suites in a historic home, then wake up to watch the porpoises cavorting offshore. In the historic district, the **Kenwood Inn** ($125 and up; 904/824-2116) at 38 Marine Street has 14 rooms in a Victorian-era hotel along the Matanzas River.

For additional listings, maps, and general information, your first stop should be the **St. Augustine visitors center** (904/825-1000 or 800/OLD-CITY), across from the Castillo.

Alligator Farm

From the heart of St. Augustine, Hwy-A1A crosses over the Matanzas River on the lovely, historic Bridge of Lions to Anastasia Island, bound for the Atlantic beaches three miles to the east. On the way to the beach, just two miles south of Old Town St. Augustine on Anastasia Boulevard (Hwy-A1A), sits one of the greatest of Florida's many tourist traps, **Alligator Farm** (daily; $21.95; 904/824-3337). Touted as the world's only complete collection of crocodil-ians, this was the first and is now one of the last of many such roadside menageries. A legitimate historical landmark, Alligator Farm is also a fun and informative place to spend some time— great for kids and anyone who finds 'gators and crocs (and turtles, iguanas, monkeys, and tropical birds, all of which are here) to be captivating creatures. Start at the largest enclosure, a mossy pond seething with hundreds of baby 'gators (which you can feed), and be sure to pay your respects to Gomek, the Alligator Farm's massive taxidermied mascot, and to Maximo, a 16-foot Aussie crocodile who's still growing ever-larger.

Across from Alligator Farm, a road turns east from Hwy-A1A to **Anastasia State Recreation Area,** the site where the stone for Castillo de San Marcos was quarried, and where in addition to beaches there's an inlet set aside for windsurfing, hiking trails through coastal hammock forests, and a nice campground (904/461-2033) amidst stately live oaks and magnolia trees.

Marineland

Eighteen miles south of St. Augustine, 35 miles north of

Daytona Beach, the original sea-creature amusement park, **Marineland** (daily except Tues.; $8; 904/471-1111) opened with a "splash" in 1938 and closed down suddenly in 1998, declaring bankruptcy after struggling for years to compete with the much-larger likes of Sea World and Disney World. Marineland, which is credited with the first performing dolphins (and with playing a key role in the sci-fi movie *Creature From the Black Lagoon*), reopened in 2005 on a much smaller scale, with an "edutainment" focus on offering intimate encounters with its famous dolphins. It sounds like a magical experience, but be warned: these Swim with a Dolphin programs cost around $200 per person—and up.

About three miles north of Marineland, on the inland side of Hwy-A1A, you can see the 16-foot-thick stone walls of **Fort Matanzas,** built by the Spanish around 1736 and never conquered. Now a national historic site, it's open for free tours.

Continuing along the coast south of Marineland, you start to see roadside fruit stands advertising "Indian River Fruit"—something you'll see more of as you travel south. This stretch of Hwy-A1A, around the town of Flagler Beach, is also one of the few where you can actually see the ocean from the road.

Daytona Beach

Offering a heady barrage of blue-collar beach culture, **Daytona Beach** (pop. 61,900) is a classic road-trip destination in every way, shape, and form. The beach here is huge—over 20 miles long, and 500 feet wide at low tide—and there's a small amusement pier at the foot of Main Street (with a Sky Ride that dangles you over the fishermen below, and a rather more dangerous "Slingshot" that hurtles riders over 300 feet, at speeds equivalent to 100 mph), but the rest of Daytona Beach is rather rough at the edges, with boarded-up shops and some lively bars and nightclubs filling the few blocks between the beach area and the Halifax River, which separates the beach from the rest of the town.

Besides being a living museum of pop

The town of **Ormond Beach,** which adjoins the north side of Daytona Beach, was also used by early speed-seekers. Prior to that, it was a winter playground of the rich and famous, richest and most famously **John D. Rockefeller,** who wintered here for years before his death in 1937 at age 97. His mansion, called **The Casements,** is now a museum (386/676-3216), along the east bank of the Halifax River at 25 Riverside Drive.

Adding to Daytona's already broad mix of pop culture icons is the **Hamburger Hall of Fame** (tours by appointment; 386/254-8753). This wacky collection of burger-related memorabilia is displayed in the private home of burgermeister Harry Sperl.

culture, Daytona Beach has long played an important role in car culture: In the first decades of the 20th century, a real Who's Who of international automotive pioneers—Henry Ford, R. E. Olds, Malford Duesenberg, and more—came here to test the upper limits of automotive performance. The first world land-speed record (a whopping 68 mph!) was set here in 1903, and by 1935 the ill-starred British racer Malcolm Campbell had raised it to 276 mph.

The speed racers later moved west to Bonneville Salt Flats in Utah, and Daytona became the breeding ground for stock car racing—today's Daytona 500 started out as a series of 100- to 200-mile races around a rough four-mile oval, half on the sands and half on a paved frontage road. The circuit races, both for cars and motorcycles, really came into their own after World War II. In 1947, NASCAR (the National Association for Stock Car Auto Racing) was founded here as the nascent sport's governing body, but the races soon outgrew the sands, and in 1958 they were moved to the purpose-built **Daytona International Speedway,** on US-92 six miles west of the beach, right off I-95 exit 87.

Daytona offers "ride-alongs" and on-track driving experiences (for a mere $150 to $2,500), but for most visitors the racing experience is brought to life at the very enjoyable **Daytona 500 Experience** ($24; 386/681-6530), part museum and part amusement park, where you can learn the history of stock car racing, take part in a simulated pit stop, play video games and motion simulators, and watch a loud and totally thrilling big screen IMAX movie, and take a bus ride around the legendary track. After a visit, you may want to spend some time practicing your skills at the **Speed Park** go-kart and drag racing track (386/253-3278) across the street.

Daytona Beach Practicalities

Daytona Beach is party central during March and April, when some 300,000 college kids escape from northern climes to defrost and unwind with a vengeance. There has been a concerted effort to keep a lid on things recently, but if you're after peace and quiet you should head somewhere else. The same is true of the springtime "Bike Week" before the Daytona 200 in March, and again in fall during "Biketoberfest," when thousands of motorcycling enthusiasts descend upon Daytona for a week or more of partying in between races at Daytona Speedway. The granddaddy of all stock car races, the Daytona 500, is held around Valentine's Day, but getting one of the 110,000 tickets is all but impossible for casual fans.

A world apart from the spring break, biker, and race car scenes, but just a mile from the beach, the **Cuban Sandwich Shop** (386/255-6655), at 722 Mason Avenue, serves inexpensive Cuban food and great fresh fruit smoothies.

There are tons of high-rise hotels along beachfront Atlantic Avenue, including the large and spacious **Holiday Inn,** 930 N. Atlantic Avenue ($125 and up; 386/255-5494). There are also a lot of low-rise motels, like the unusual **Traveler's Inn** ($45–60; 386/253-3501) at 735 N. Atlantic Avenue, where the rooms are all decorated with murals of movie stars (from Marilyn Monroe to John Wayne) and biker chicks.

The Space Coast: Cape Canaveral

It's more than a little ironic that one of the most extensive sections of natural coastal wetlands left in Florida is home to the launch pads of the nation's space program. Though the natural aspects— thousands of seabirds and wide open stretches of sandy beaches—are attractive enough in their own right to merit a visit, most people are drawn here because the undeveloped landscape allows clear and generally unobstructed views of missile launches and Space Shuttle take-offs and landings, at Cape Canaveral's **Kennedy Space Center.** All the big milestones in the history of the U.S. space program—the Mercury, Gemini, Apollo, and Space Shuttle launches—happened here,

To watch a space shuttle or other launch at Kennedy Space Center, you can get passes from the visitors center, or simply watch from the many good vantage points: **Playalinda Beach,** in the Canaveral National Seashore at the west end of Hwy-402 from Titusville; across the Indian River, along US-1 in Titusville; or the beaches west of Hwy-A1A in **Cocoa Beach.**

and if names like Alan Shepard, John Glenn, or Neil Armstrong mean anything to you, set aside time for a visit.

The Kennedy Space Center itself, eight miles west of US-1 via the NASA Parkway (Hwy-405), is open to the public, but only on guided tours. These tours require advance tickets, and all leave from the large **visitors complex** (daily; $18–38; 866/737-5235) where a pair of IMAX theaters show films of outer space to get you in the mood. There are also some small museums, a simulated Space Shuttle mission control center, a half dozen missiles in the Rocket Garden, and an actual Space Shuttle, which you can walk through. The visitors center also has a couple of fast-food restaurants and a kennel for pets.

At the entrance to the Kennedy Space Center visitors center, the **Astronaut Memorial** is a huge black granite block backed by high-tech mirrors that reflect sunlight onto the surface of the stone, illuminating the engraved names of the men and women who have given their lives exploring space.

To see the Kennedy Space Center up close, board a bus for a tour; these leave every few minutes and visit the Apollo and Space Shuttle launch pads and other sites, including a mock-up of the International Space Station. On other tours, you can visit the Cape Canaveral Air Force station or the Cape Canaveral Air Station, site of many early "Space Race" adventures, or even have lunch with an astronaut and talk about outer space with someone who's actually been there (glass of Tang not included).

One of the best places to eat in this part of Florida is west of the Space Center, in the town of Titusville: **Dixie Crossroads** (daily; 321/268-5000), at 1475 Garden Street, an immense (and immensely popular) place to eat seafood, especially massive plates of shrimp. All-you-can-eat piles of small shrimp cost $20, while jumbo shrimp cost around $1 apiece. The Crossroads is away from the water, two miles east of I-95 exit 220.

Cocoa Beach

The town of Cocoa Beach, familiar to anyone who ever watched the 1960s Space Age sitcom *I Dream of Jeannie,* sits south of the Kennedy Space Center, and the town pier that juts out into the Atlantic Ocean at the north end of town is a prime spot for viewing Space Shuttle and other rocket launches. Long before there were Space Shuttles, or even NASA, Cocoa Beach was home to the Cape Canaveral Air Station, the launch site for the unmanned space probes of the late 1950s, including the

East from Hwy-A1A on the south side of Cocoa Beach, **"I Dream of Jeannie Lane"** leads down to a nice beachfront park.

first U.S. satellite (Explorer 1), and the famous "astro chimps" (Gordo, Able, and Miss Baker, who were sent into orbit to test the effects of weightlessness). The Air Station, which is accessible through the Kennedy Space Center complex, has historical exhibits and dozens of missiles, from today's Patriots back to German V2s (which were fired at England during World War II and provided the engineering basis for the American rockets of a decade later). The on-site museum includes early computers and other equipment, housed inside the blockhouse from which the first launches were controlled.

Though travel to outer space is clearly on the minds of many residents, especially personnel stationed at Patrick Air Force Base here, another focus is catching the perfect wave: Cocoa Beach is surf center of the Space Coast. Along with a clean, 10-mile-long beach, the town also holds a batch of

good-value motels, located within a short walk of the waves. Choose from chains (including a Motel 6), or check out the garish pink **Fawlty Towers** ($85 and up; 321/784-3870), at 100 E. Cocoa Beach Causeway (Hwy-520), which for fans of the eponymous British sit-com is sadly devoid of John Cleese or put-upon Juan. It is, however, walkably close to the beach, and right next door to Cocoa Beach's main event, the massive **Ron Jon Surf Shop** (321/799-8888), open 24 hours every day at 4151 Atlantic Avenue, and *the* place to buy or rent surfboards, body boards, or bicycles.

Vero Beach

As a boy growing up in sunny Los Angeles, I could never understand why the Dodgers felt they had to disappear to distant Florida to get in shape during Spring Training. I knew the weather couldn't be so much better there (after all, didn't L.A. have the heavenly climate?), and I never quite figured out what

Detour: Orlando and Walt Disney World

Entire guidebooks are devoted to covering the mind-boggling array of tourist attractions in and around Orlando, but three words would probably suffice: **Walt Disney World.** Over 50,000 people come here every day to experience the magic of the Magic Kingdom, which is divided into four main areas—the Magic Kingdom amusement park, a new Animal Kingdom animal park, the futuristic EPCOT Center, and the Disney-MGM studio tours. Entrance to any of these will set you back around $80; to see all of them, get a "park-hopper" pass, which is valid for four days (about $225) or longer. For further information on admissions and lodging packages call 407/824-4321.

At the time of writing, there's still no law that says you have to go to Disney World just because you've come to Florida, but it is a cultural phenomenon and more than a little fun. For a Disneyfied view of the ideal American town, visit the Walt Disney Company's retro-Victorian planned community of **Celebration** (pop. 9,000 and growing), south of US-192 at the I-4 junction. Contrary to popular belief, this is not the town seen in the Jim Carrey movie *The Truman Show* (that was Seaside, in the Florida Panhandle), but it could have been.

While you're in Orlando, you may want to visit other big-time attractions like Sea World and Universal Studios, but there are also some funky, pre–Disney era tourist

the big attraction of Vero Beach, the Dodgers' historic off-season home, could be. But when I discovered that the Dodgers had started playing here way back in 1948—back when they still called Brooklyn home—it all began to make sense. But all that is now in the past—after 60 years, the Dodgers moved west to Arizona in 2008, and the managers of **Dodgertown,** their former training complex, are looking for a new tenant.

traps, with ad budgets small enough that you won't have to fight the crowds. Best of this bunch is probably **GatorLand,** 14501 S. Orange Blossom Trail (daily; $24; 407/855-5496), where thousands of alligators, crocodiles, snakes, and other reptiles are gathered together in a cypress swamp. You enter through a gator's gaping jaws, and inside you can see such sights as live chickens being dangled over a pond, taunting the hungry carnivorous gators just of out reach below. Continuing south along US-441, past the world headquarters of Tupperware, another sight of offbeat interest is the 100-year-old historic district at the heart of **Kissimmee** (pop. 38,200), where a 50-foot stone and concrete pyramid, constructed in 1943 with rocks from most states, as well as 21 countries, stands in Lake Front Park.

It doesn't take a Boy Genius to figure out the customer base of the Jimmy Neutron–themed **Nickelodeon Family Suites** ($125 and up; 877/642-5111), kid-friendly Holiday Inn with multiple bedroom suites (and a fun but chaotic pool area—avoid the holiday peak times) near Disney World. Another movie spinoff: Disney's extraordinary **Animal Kingdom Lodge** (around $250; 407/939-6244), where a 30-acre savannah landscape, complete with roaming giraffes and zebras you can see from your balconies, offers families and fans of *The Lion King* the chance to take an African safari—without the jet lag.

Between Orlando and the Space Coast, the Beeline Expressway (Hwy-528) is a fast, flat toll road, with only three exits in the 30 miles between I-95 and greater Orlando.

With or without baseball, Vero Beach is a really nice place, with an excellent beach, in South Beach Park at the end of the Palmetto Causeway. This South Beach is family-friendly and about as far as you can get from Miami's South Beach and still be in Florida: the sands here are clean, grainy, and golden, the waves are good-sized, and there are showers and free parking. Vero Beach also has a nice place to stay and eat: the **Driftwood Resort** (772/231-0550) at 3150 Ocean Drive, which has funky 1950s-style motel rooms, and the fun and good-value **Waldo's,** a poolside café and bar overlooking the ocean.

Spring Training: Grapefruit League Baseball

Every February and March, hundreds of baseball players at all levels of expertise head to Florida to earn or keep their places on some 20 different major league teams and their minor league farm club affiliates. The informality and ease of access during this spring training, which is known as the Grapefruit League, attracts thousands of baseball fans as well. Though they're not necessarily played to win, Grapefruit League games are played in modern 10,000-seat stadia that approach the major leagues in quality, and the smaller size allows an up-close feel you'd have to pay much more for during the regular season. (And your chances of snagging balls during batting practice, or the early morning training sessions, are infinitely better, too.)

Most of the Grapefruit League teams make their springtime homes on the Gulf Coast, but many others locate in cities and towns along Florida's Atlantic coast, and some teams are in the Orlando area, including the Atlanta Braves and the Houston Astros. The teams move around from town to town depending on the deals they can finagle from local taxpayers, but at time of writing, the New York Mets train in Port St. Lucie, the Washington Nationals in the Space Coast town of Viera, while the St. Louis Cardinals and Florida Marlins play in Jupiter.

Fort Pierce and Jupiter

South of Vero Beach, Hwy-A1A continues along North Hutchinson Island past the **UDT Navy SEALs Museum** (closed Mon.; $6; 772/595-5845), which describes the various roles played by underwater divers in demolishing enemy property during wartime. Among the displays of wetsuits and explosives is an Apollo capsule—it's Navy SEALs who rescued returning astronauts after they "splashed down" in the ocean. On either side of the museum, undeveloped stretches of the coast have been preserved in a pair of

South of Fort Pierce, Port St. Lucie is the spring training home of the **New York Mets** (772/871-2115), who play at 525 NW Peacock Boulevard, off I-95.

parks, where you can enjoy uncrowded beaches or wander along boardwalks through thickly forested mangrove swamps.

Bending inland across the North Bridge, Hwy-A1A links up briefly with US-1, the old Dixie Highway, through the town of **Fort Pierce** (pop. 37,516), a market center of the famous "Indian River" produce-growing district. After this half-mile detour, Hwy-A1A returns to the shore, passing along the way by the very good **St. Lucie County Historical Museum** (closed Mon.; $4), at the east end of the South Bridge, where broad-ranging displays tell the history of the region, showing off a hand-carved canoe and explaining the "fort" in Fort Pierce (it was built in 1835, during the Seminole Wars).

South of Fort Pierce, Hwy-A1A embarks on a nearly 30-mile run along Hutchinson Island, where dense stands of pines block the views of largely undeveloped beachfront. On the coast just north of Palm Beach, the town of **Jupiter** has a landmark lighthouse, which you can climb inside up to the top for a grand view, and Roger Dean Stadium is spring training home of the Marlins and Cardinals, as well as their Class A Florida League farm clubs. Pop culture fans may also want to know that Jupiter has long been home to movie star Burt Reynolds: his achievements (from TV's *Gunsmoke* through movies like *Deliverance* and *Smokey and the Bandit*) are chronicled at his acting school and museum, at 100 N. US-1 (Fri.–Sun.; $5; 561/743-9955), though redevelopment threatens to leave Burt's museum and school without a home.

Palm Beach

A South Florida sibling to the conspicuous consumption that once defined Newport, Rhode Island, **Palm Beach** (pop. 10,468) has been a winter refuge for the rich and famous since Henry Flagler started work on his fashionable (but long-vanished) resort hotel, the 1,150-room Royal Poinciana. It was the world's largest wood building when completed in 1894, but the site is now an upscale shopping district at the center of town. Away from here, most of Palm Beach is well-guarded private property, off-limits to most mere mortals. The best way for anyone not named

Inland from Palm Beach, you can wave at rhinos, lions, and wildebeest in a 500-acre, drive-through simulation of African ecosystems at **Lion Country Safari** (561/793-1084), 18 miles west of I-95 via US-98. No convertibles allowed!

The town of **Lantana,** on the coast between Palm Beach and Boca Raton, is the home of the National Enquirer tabloid.

Kennedy or Pierpont to get a look at Palm Beach life is to spend some time at the Hearst Castle of the East Coast, the **Henry Morrison Flagler Museum** (closed Mon.; $18; 561/655-2833), on the inland side of downtown Palm Beach, at the north end of Cocoanut Row. Officially known as Whitehall, this opulent 60,000-square-foot mansion was Flagler's private home, and the 50-plus rooms (many of which were taken from European buildings and re-installed here) contain historical exhibits tracing the life of Flagler, the Standard Oil baron (John D. Rockefeller's right-hand man) who made a fortune while making Florida into an immensely popular vacation destination.

Even bigger and better than Whitehall is **The Breakers,** a stately resort hotel that faces the ocean at the east end of Palm Beach and retains much of its 1920s Mediterranean style and grace. Rooms will set you back around $350 a night (much more for suites), but you can enjoy the lobby, have a drink or afternoon tea, or take a tour (Wed. at 3 PM only; free; 561/655-6611).

Not surprisingly, there are some very good and very expensive restaurants in and around Palm Beach, but happily there's also a very nice, normal, all-American luncheonette just two blocks north of The Breakers: **Green's Pharmacy,** 151 N. County Road (561/832-4443), serving very good diner-style meals.

Boca Raton

Whoever named **Boca Raton** (pop. 74,764), which translates literally as "Rat's Mouth," clearly didn't have an ear for future promotional bonanza, but despite the awkward name the town has become one of the more chichi spots in the state. As in Palm Beach, Coral Gables, and Miami's South Beach, the best of Boca dates from the 1920s, when architect and real estate promoter Addison Mizner, flush from his success building Mediterranean-style manors in Palm Beach, created a mini Venice of resorts and canals, which survives mainly in the shocking pink palazzo of the **Boca Raton Resort** ($200 and up; 561/447-3000), on the southeast side of town at 501 E. Camino Royal.

Downtown Boca has been turned into a massive stucco shopping mall, but it's worth braving for a look inside the ornate Mizner-designed Town Hall, on US-1 (old Dixie Highway) in Palmetto Park downtown, which now houses the local historical museum (closed Mon.; free).

US-1, the main route through town, also holds the very

popular **Boca Diner** (561/750-6744), serving above-average coffee shop fare at 2801 N. Federal Highway; the early evening "Early Bird" scene here is straight out of *Seinfeld*.

Hwy-A1A misses most of Boca Raton, cruising past along the densely pine-forested coast. The beaches are accessible but hard to find; one well-marked stop along the way is the **Gumbo Limbo Nature Center** (Mon.–Sat. 9 AM–4 PM, Sun. noon–4 PM; $3 donation; 561/338-1473) on the inland side of the highway, a mile north of Mizner Park. A variety of native Floridian landscapes have been re-created here, letting you wander at will past coastal dunes, mangrove wetlands, and rare sabal palm hammocks. Across Hwy-A1A, **Red Reef Park** is a popular surfing beach.

Fort Lauderdale

Once famed for wild spring break frolics that saw thousands of college kids descending here for an orgy of drunken round-the-clock partying, **Fort Lauderdale** (pop. 162,800) is a surprisingly residential city, brought to a more human scale by the many waterways that cut through it. One of the largest cargo ports in the state, Fort Lauderdale also boasts more boats per capita than just about anywhere else in the United States, and over 165 miles of canals, inlets, and other waterways flow through the city.

Fort Lauderdale is said to be one of the points that form the **Bermuda Triangle,** so of course there are numerous beachside bars where college kids try to simulate its supernatural effects by imbibing too many margaritas.

Downtown Fort Lauderdale has a few big, dull office towers, but along the New River there are some well-preserved historic buildings dating back to 1905, when the city first emerged from the swamps. Find out more by visiting the **Historical Museum** (Tues.–Fri. 10 AM–4 PM; $10), west of US-1 at 231 S.W. 2nd Avenue, which has lots of old photos and walking-tour maps, or the nifty **Stranahan House** (daily; $12), off Las Olas Blvd. at 335 S.E. 6th Avenue, a circa-1901 trading post and house, with broad verandas and a high ceiling to help cool down in the days before air-conditioning. Still owned by the same family that built it, the Stranahan House is one of the most evocative historic places in the state.

Fort Lauderdale's main beachfront bar and nightclub district is along Atlantic Avenue and Las Olas Boulevard, where you'll find some nice sidewalk cafés and fast-food restaurants. One culinary landmark: **Johnny V.'s,** 625 E. Las Olas

(954/761-7920), a popular and stylish haunt where traditional American dishes are enlivened by a canny blend of exotic ingredients. For a change of pace from the frenetic tourism, or simply to enjoy good basic fried seafood, cold beer, and live blues, head south down US-1 to **Ernie's BBQ Lounge** (954/523-8636) at 1843 S. Federal Highway, famous for its conch fritters, calamari rings, and rooftop deck.

Miles of inexpensive motels line Hwy-A1A north of Fort Lauderdale, and unless there's something big going on you shouldn't have trouble finding a room for under $100—half that in summer. One of the nicest places is the moderately priced, family-friendly **TropiRock Resort,** 2900 Belmar Street ($80 and up; 954/564-0523), with tennis courts, a tiki bar, and a pool, just a short walk from the beach.

North of Fort Lauderdale, Hwy-A1A winds in along the coast through a series of funky, friendly beachside communities. South of Fort Lauderdale, Hwy-A1A heads inland and merges into US-1, returning to the coast for the run south to Miami Beach.

North Miami Beach

Between Fort Lauderdale and Miami Beach, Hwy-A1A runs along the shore, first as Ocean Drive and later as Collins Avenue, while US-1 runs inland parallel to (and sometimes as) the old Dixie Highway. There's nothing here to compare with the attractions farther south, but the town of **North Miami Beach** does have one oddity: the **Ancient Spanish Monastery** (hours vary; 305/945-1461), at 16711 W. Dixie Highway, a 12th-century monastery bought in the 1920s by William Randolph Hearst, who had it dismantled and shipped to the United States for his "Hearst Castle" complex in California. However, after the stones were confiscated by U.S. Customs and Hearst lost his fortune in the Great Depression, the monastery was finally rebuilt here in Florida—as an Episcopal church.

On the coast, Hwy-A1A runs past a number of indistinct beach towns before hitting **Bal Harbour,** home to one of Miami's biggest and best shopping malls, and one of its biggest beaches, **Haulover Beach.** From here south to Miami Beach, the road is lined with towering concrete condos and hotels.

Miami Beach

Covering a broad island separating downtown Miami from the open Atlantic Ocean, **Miami Beach** (pop. 87,933) has long

Carl Fisher: Father of Miami Beach

Fisher Park, on the bay side of Miami Beach on Alton Road at 51st Street, holds a small monument to the fascinating Carl Fisher, the man most responsible for turning Miami Beach from a mangrove swamp into America's favorite resort. Before building up Lincoln Avenue into Miami Beach's first commercial district, Carl Fisher had played an important role in America's early automotive history. Called the "P. T. Barnum of the Automobile Age," Fisher made millions through the Prest-O-Lite company, which in the early 1900s developed the first functioning car headlight. Around 1910, he invested this fortune in building and promoting the Indianapolis Motor Speedway, then went on to plan and publicize both the Lincoln Highway, America's first transcontinental road, and the Dixie Highway, the first main north–south route in the eastern United States. He invested heavily in Miami Beach property but was ruined by the Great Depression and the sudden drop in land values. He died here, nearly penniless, in 1939, just as the economy was rebounding and the art deco hotels of South Beach were bringing new life to Miami Beach.

been a mecca for fans of 1930s art deco architecture and design. More recently, it's also become one of the world's most fashionable and bacchanalian beach resorts, with deluxe hotels and high-style nightclubs and restaurants lining the broad white sands of South Beach, the relatively small corner of Miami Beach that gets 99 percent of the press and tourist attention. Here, along beachfront Ocean Drive and busier Collins Avenue (Hwy-A1A) a block inland, you'll find dozens of glorious art deco hotels, many lighted with elegant neon signs. Guided walking tours (Wed.–Sun.; $20) of the district leave from the **Art Deco Gift Shop**

The stately Mediterranean Revival manor where fashion designer **Gianni Versace** lived and was murdered sits at the heart of South Beach, on Ocean Drive just north of 11th Street.

Miami

Equal parts jet-set glitz and multicultural grit, and with more than half its population coming here from other countries around the globe, Miami (pop. 372,000) really embodies the transitive state of the nation in the early years of the 21st century. Having sprung up from swampland in the 1920s, Miami has weathered hurricanes and race riots, real estate booms and busts, drug running, and endless political intrigue to become one of America's most energetic cities. In her 1987 book *Miami,* Joan Didion describes the city as an economically schizophrenic place where it's possible "to pass from walled enclaves to utter desolation while changing stations on the car radio."

Approaching from Miami Beach past the cruise ship docks along the MacArthur Causeway, or the older and more leisurely Venetian Causeway, you experience the view of Miami made famous by the 1980s television series *Miami Vice*—downtown towers rising above Biscayne Bay. West of downtown, Miami's most engaging district is Little Havana, which focuses along SW 8th Street (a.k.a. Calle Ocho) between 12th and 16th Avenues. Since the 1950s and 1960s, when the first refugees fleeing Castro's regime fetched up here, this neighborhood has been the heart of Cuban-American Miami. The Latin American influence on Miami is evident everywhere you go, but for proof of just how deep the connections run, consider the fact that two of Cuba's deposed presidents, Gerardo Machado and Carlos Prio, are buried in Miami's Woodlawn Park Cemetery, a mile west of Little Havana. Former Nicaraguan dictator Anastasio Somoza is buried there, too. Hang out for a while with the old men who congregate in the Domino Park on 8th Street and 14th Avenue, or visit the "Martyrs of Giron" (a.k.a. Bay of Pigs) Monument along 8th Street between 12th and 13th Streets; you'll definitely get a feel for it. Better yet, stop for something to eat or drink at one of Little Havana's many great Cuban cafes, like **Versailles** (305/444-0240), at 3555 SW 8th Street, a favorite haunt of Miami's politically potent anti-Castro Cuban-Americans.

Enjoy very good, very traditional Cuban food: a bowl of *ropa vieja* (tender threads of garlicky beef in a black bean soup), finished off with a creamy flan and a cup of super-strong Cuban coffee.

For an entirely different aspect of Miami, check out the two-time wild card World Series champion **Florida Marlins** (305/930-4487), who play at Land Shark Stadium, 16 miles north of Miami at 2267 NW 199th Street.

Miami Beach has the best range of stylish hotels, but in downtown Miami the characterful and historic **Miami River Inn** ($70–199; 305/325-0045) is a well-preserved circa-1908 hotel with B&B rooms (all with private baths) in a slightly questionable neighborhood at 118 SW South River Drive. At the top end of the style and expense spectrum is the **Four Seasons** ($350 and up; 305/358-3535) at 1435 Brickell Avenue, offering stunning views from a 64-story tower. Back down to earth, the major chains all have locations on the downtown waterfront; as at all South Florida accommodations, room rates tend to increase considerably during the peak season (Jan.–Apr.).

The best source of information on greater Miami, including Miami Beach, is the **Greater Miami visitors bureau** (305/539-3000 or 800/933-8448) at 701 Brickell Avenue.

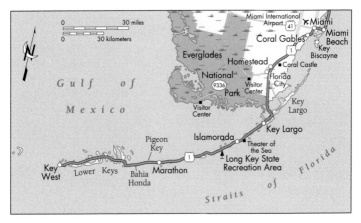

(daily; 305/672-2014) at 1200 Ocean Drive, which also rents iPod-based self-guided tours and sells guidebooks, posters, postcards, and anything else you can think of that has to do with the art deco era.

No matter how intoxicating the architecture, beach life, and nightlife along South Beach are, while you're here be sure to set aside an hour or two to explore the fascinating collection of pop culture artifacts on display two blocks inland at the **Wolfsonian** (closed Wed.; $7; 305/531-1001), at 1001 Washington Avenue. One of the odder highbrow museums you'll find, the Wolfsonian (officially the Mitchell Wolfson Jr. Collection of Decorative and Propaganda Arts) fills a retrofitted 1920s warehouse with four floors of furniture, sculpture, architectural models, posters, and much more, almost all dating from the "Modern Era," roughly 1885 to 1945. Two areas of excellence are drawings and murals created under the New Deal auspices of the WPA, and similar agitprop artifacts created in Weimar, Germany. Only a small portion of the extensive collection is on display at any one time, and most of the floor space is given over to changing exhibitions—on anything from World's Fairs to Florida tourism to how children's books were used to indoctrinate future soldiers—but it's a thought-provoking and surprisingly fun place, with an unexpressed but overriding theme of how art can counterbalance, or at least respond to, the demands of industrial society.

Miami Beach Practicalities

Not surprisingly, there are scores of cafés and restaurants in and around Miami Beach; some, like exotic **Wish** (305/674-9474) in The Hotel at 801 Collins Avenue, are rated among the best in the world. More down to earth, and just two blocks west of the beach, the **11th Street Diner** (305/534-6373) on 11th and Washington is a 1948 Paramount pre-fab diner, plunked down in 1992 and open 24 hours ever since.

For an unforgettably hedonistic experience, check into one of South Beach's great old art deco hotels, or at least saunter through the lobby and stop for a drink. The **Delano,** 1685 Collins Avenue ($350 and up; 305/672-2000), is a high-style, Shrager/Starck symphony in white; while the **Raleigh,** 1775 Collins Avenue ($250 and up; 305/534-6300), has the coolest pool in South Beach—and that is really saying something. Dozens of these 1930s divas stand out along Ocean Drive and Collins Avenue, but the wonderful architecture, alas, doesn't always manage to mask their elderly bones, nor is the 24-hour hubbub that surrounds them especially conducive to a good night's sleep. Ocean Drive, by the way, is undriveable on weekend nights, since so many cars cruise up and down it, stereos blasting.

Stylish though it is, South Beach is not frequented by many locals, who instead tend to spend time on **Lincoln Road,** a half mile north of South Beach. The Mediterranean Revival–style commercial district along Lincoln Road, developed in the 1920s by promoter Carl Fisher, was the original main drag of Miami Beach; it has been pedestrianized and nicely landscaped and is now packed with dozens of lively sidewalk cafés. Japanese refinement meets Brazilian passions at the iconoclastic **Sushi Samba Dromo** (305/673-5337), a fish lovers' paradise at 600 Lincoln Road.

Across Miami

The I-95 freeway, and the old main route, US-1, both enter Miami north of downtown in the very rough Little Haiti neighborhood, while the infinitely more scenic Hwy-A1A crosses Biscayne Bay from Miami Beach. Around downtown, Biscayne Boulevard winds along the waterfront, merging into historic Brickell Avenue, now lined by flashy postmodern bank and condo towers. From here, detour west on the one-way system along 7th and 8th Streets through Little Havana, then south through Coral Gables, joining the old Dixie Highway (US-1) for the drive south through Homestead to the Florida Keys.

Coral Gables

South of Miami's Little Havana neighborhood, accessible through grand gates off the Tamiami Trail (8th Street), the stately community of **Coral Gables** is one of the few Florida resort towns that survives fairly unchanged since the boom years of the 1920s. Coral Gables boasts many grand boulevards, fine fountains, plazas, and lush gardens, but the landmark to look for is the 26-story **Biltmore Hotel** ($350 and up; 305/445-1926 or 800/727-1926), at 1200 Anastasia Avenue off Granada Boulevard. This opulent hotel, which opened in 1926 and once boasted the world's largest swimming pool (Johnny Weismuller was the original lifeguard!), has been restored to its original glory.

In 1983, the Bulgarian artist **Christo** wrapped 11 Biscayne Bay islands in bright pink plastic as part of his Surrounded Islands installation.

The southern edge of Coral Gables is occupied by the drab campus of the University of Miami, which is bounded by US-1, the old Dixie Highway.

Homestead: Coral Castle

One of the most diverting stops between Miami and the Florida Keys has to be the **Coral Castle,** 28655 S. Dixie Highway (daily; $10; 305/248-6345), an amazing house hand-carved out of huge blocks of oolitic coral in the 1930s. Located right along the highway, two miles north of Homestead, the house is filled with furniture also carved from stone—a 3,000-pound sofa and a 500-pound rocking chair—and no one has figured how its enigmatic creator (Ed Leedskalnin) did it all without help or the use of any heavy machinery.

Homestead, along with neighboring Florida City farther south, forms the main gateway to Everglades National Park, and there are tons of reasonably priced motels hereabouts—all the usual suspects line up here along US-1, including the very nice **Best Western Gateway to the Keys** ($90 and up; 305/246-5100).

Florida's other big national park, **Biscayne National Park,** stretches east of Homestead from near Miami to the top of the Florida Keys, but it is almost completely underwater. Privately run snorkeling and diving tours (around $30–35) leave from near the main **Convoy Point visitors center** (305/230-7275), nine miles east of US-1 at the end of 328th Street—near the huge Homestead Motorsports Complex (and a nuclear power plant).

Everglades National Park

Covering over 1.5 million acres at the far southwestern tip of mainland Florida, **Everglades National Park** protects the largest subtropical wilderness in the United States. A fair portion of the park is actually underwater, and the entire Everglades ecosystem is basically a giant, slow-flowing river that is 50 miles wide but only a few inches deep. Fed by Lake Okechobee, and under constant threat by irrigation inflows and out-flows and by the redirection of water to Miami and other cities, the Everglades still seem to vibrate with life. Some 300 species of birds breed here, as do 600 different kinds of fish and animals, ranging from rare manatees to abundant alligators (not to mention the gazillions of mosquitoes).

In the Everglades, and anywhere in Florida, **mosquitoes** are intensely annoying pests, so if you're here at any time but the dry middle of winter, bring strong insect repellent–and lots of it. In parts of the Everglades, the bugs are so bad that full-body cover is recommended, in addition to the most potent sprays and lotions you can lay your hands on.

The backcountry parts of the Everglades can be visited by boat, but by road there are only two main routes. In the north, the Tamiami Trail (the "Tampa to Miami Trail," a.k.a. US-41) heads west from Miami to misnamed **Shark Valley,** where you can rent bikes or take a tram tour ($17) on a 15-mile loop through the sawgrass swamps that make up the heart of the Everglades. Gazing at the gators, eagles, and hawks here, it's hard to believe you're barely a half hour from South Beach. Just west of Shark Valley, the **Miccosukee Indian Village** is a reminder of the Everglades native peoples, the Seminoles, some of whom now wrestle alligators, run souvenir shops, and give airboat tours of their ancestral lands.

The main road access to the Everglades is via Palm Drive (Hwy-9336) from the Florida Turnpike or US-1. This route takes you past the main **visitors center** (305/242-7700), where interpretive displays and a pair of nature trails give an appetizing taste of the Everglades (and almost guaranteed sightings of alligators). The road continues nearly 40 miles west to the former town of Flamingo, where both the residents and the namesake birds have all moved on, and the Everglades' only eating and accommodation option, the Flamingo Lodge, closed after suffering damage in the 2005 Katrina hurricane.

The Overseas Highway

Imagine a narrow ribbon of asphalt and concrete hovering between emerald seas and azure blue skies, and lined by swaying palm trees and gorgeous, white-sand beaches. Add a generous taste of exotic wildlife, including alligators and dolphins, the country's only tropical coral reefs, and a romantic history rich with tales of buccaneering pirates and buried treasure. Hang it off the far southern tip of Florida, and you have the Overseas Highway, one of the country's most fascinating scenic drives.

Running for over 125 miles from the Everglades to the edge of the Caribbean, the Overseas Highway is the southernmost section of US-1, the historic route that winds for over 2,400 miles along the full length of the East Coast. From its very inception, the Overseas Highway has been unique. It was built on top of the legendary Florida and East Coast Railroad, which at the turn of the 20th century linked the great resort hotels of St. Augustine and Palm Beach with Key West and Cuba. An engineering masterpiece, the railroad cost $50 million and hundreds of lives to complete in 1912, but it lasted only two decades before the century's most powerful hurricane destroyed the tracks in 1935. The state of Florida

Key Largo is home to the **Key Lime Products** store (305/853-0378) at milemarker 95.2, selling all manner of key lime pies, juice, cakes, cookies, suntan lotions—even key lime trees, though commercial key lime orchards are a thing of the past. (Most key limes today come from Mexico and Honduras.)

Key Largo

The Overseas Highway (US-1) officially starts in Florida City, near the Everglades some 50 miles south of Miami, but doesn't really come alive until it leaves the mainland and lands at **Key Largo,** the first and largest of the dozens of "keys" (from the Spanish word *cayos,* meaning small islands) the highway links together. The Overseas Highway reaches Key Largo at the very popular **John** bought the remnants of the railroad for $650,000 and proceeded to convert it into a two-lane highway, the Overseas Highway, which opened to traffic in 1938. Most of the old road has since been superseded by a more modern highway, but many old bridges and causeways still stand as evocative remnants of an earlier era.

As in much of Florida, ramshackle roadside development has uglified much of the route—in the larger Keys towns, like Key Largo, Islamorada, and Marathon, signs hawking restaurants, motels, and snorkel tours are more common than pelicans—but you can't help but be hypnotized by the scenic beauty of what pockets of nature still remain. Many of the best views are from the road itself, and specifically from the bridges, such as the Long Key Bridge and soaring Seven Mile Bridge, which run north and south of Marathon. Two state parks, John Pennecamp on Key Largo and Bahia Honda in the Lower Keys, offer a respite from the commercialism, and all along the Overseas Highways, unmarked roads and driveways lead across the narrow keys down to the waterside, where all manner of sportfishing marinas and Margaritaville-type bars give you another outlook on the true "Key experience."

All the way along the Overseas Highway (US-1), the roadside is lined by milemarker posts counting down the miles from Florida City to Key West, starting at MM 127 and ending up at MM 0; addresses usually make reference to these numbers. Though it's only about 160 miles, be sure to allow at least four hours for the drive between Miami and Key West—plus however many hours you manage to spend out of the car, of course.

Pennecamp Coral Reef State Park (daily; $4; 305/451-1202), at MM 102.5. The first place where you can really get a feel for life on the Keys, the park is the starting point for a variety of **guided tours** (scuba diving, snorkeling, or in glass-bottomed boats) that offer up-close looks at the only tropical coral reef in the continental United States, and all but guarantee that you'll see enough sealife to fill a photo album or two. Along with the adjacent **Key Largo Coral Reef National Marine Sanctuary,** the park gives access to more than 175 square miles of diving spots, including reefs, shipwrecks, and a nine-foot-high bronze statue called *Christ of the Deep.* The visitors center has a replica reef in a 30,000-gallon aquarium full of colorful fish, allowing a quick look at the fascinating underwater world without getting your feet wet; the park also has other on-land attractions, like a boardwalk over a mangrove swamp and a pleasant campground.

> Between milemarker 106 and milemarker 86, a hiking and bicycling path parallels US-1—sometimes very closely—but it's a rare long-distance route on these tiny islands.

Film fans will know that Key Largo was the title and setting of a great 1948 film noir movie starring Bogie, Bacall, and Edward G. Robinson; these days, it's also home to the co-star of another classic, the boat from the *African Queen,* which is moored next to the Holiday Inn at MM 100. Most of Key Largo today, however, is a rather tawdry four-mile stretch of seashell stands, dive shops, boat shops, and margarita bars; there are many good restaurants, including **Mrs. Mac's Kitchen** (305/451-3722) at MM 99.4, a small and friendly place with inexpensive food all day, and more beers to drink than seats to sit on.

Key Largo also has many good places to stay, from the funky **Sunset Cove Motel** ($125 and up; 305/451-0705) at MM 99.5, to the boutique **Azul del Mar** ($175 and up; 305/451-0337), a relaxing small resort at MM 104.3. Also here: the unique **Jules' Undersea Lodge** (packages from $300 per person; 305/451-2353), a two-room motel that's 22 feet beneath the sea—a quick scuba dive down from 51 Shoreland Drive, off MM 103.2.

Islamorada

Continuing south on US-1, Key Largo blends into **Islamorada** (EYE-la-mo-RA-da), the self-proclaimed "Sportfishing Capital of the World," where anglers from all over the world come to try their hands at catching the elusive, hard-fighting bonefish that dwell in the shallow saltwater "flats," and the deep-sea tarpon, marlin, and sailfish. Though now famous for its fishing and fun-in-the-sun, Islamorada (Purple Island) used to be synonymous with death and destruction: On September 2, 1935, a huge tsunami, whipped up by 200-mile-per-hour hurricane winds, drowned over 400 refugees trying to escape on what turned out to be the last train ever to travel along the old Florida East Coast Railway. Most of the dead were WW I veterans, members of the "Bonus Army" who had marched on Washington, D.C., in 1934 and had been given jobs working to build the Overseas Highway. A stone pillar at the south end of Islamorada, along US-1 at MM 81.6, was erected by the WPA to remember the event.

At the center of Islamorada sits one of the older tourist traps in south Florida: the **Theater of the Sea** (daily; $25; 305/664-2431), at MM 84.5, a funky, friendly place where you can watch performing sea animals or even swim with dolphins.

Islamorada is also home to what may be the most pleasant and plushest accommodation option in the Florida Keys: **The Moorings** ($250 and up; 305/664-4708), on the ocean side of MM 81.5 at 123 Beach Road. The Moorings is an idyllic and much-loved retreat, with 18 self-sufficient wooden cottages on 18 acres, alongside a beautiful 1,100-foot white sand beach.

There are a number of places in the Florida Keys where you can pay to swim with dolphins, including: **Dolphins Plus** (866/860-7946) in Key Largo; **Theatre of the Sea** (305/664-2431) in Islamorada; and the **Dolphin Research Center** (305/289-0002) in Marathon. Each charges around $150 (and up!) for a short but memorable swim.

The Moorings also has a nice restaurant, **Morada Bay,** serving urbane renditions of traditional Key favorites on US-1 at MM 81.6. For a more down-to-earth taste of the Keys, try the nearby **Green Turtle Inn** (305/664-2006).

For more information on Islamorada, stop by the little red caboose (at MM 82.5) that holds the **visitors bureau** (305/664-4503 or 800/322-5397). Outside, in the parking lot, informational plaques tell the story of the ill-fated railroad that became the **Overseas Highway.**

Long Key State Park

South of Islamorada, up and over the high "Channel 5" bridge, the roadside scene gets pretty again very fast, especially at the **Long Key State Park** at MM 67.5, where boardwalks wind through coastal "hammocks"—dense stands of mahogany and dogwood trees that bunch together on the small humps of land that lie above the tide line. There's a **campground** ($36; 305/664-4815) in the park, with showers, and some nice but narrow beaches.

Marathon and Pigeon Key

The second-longest of the many bridges that make up US-1, the elegant multi-arched Long Key Bridge supports a long, flat causeway where the road finally earns its other name, the Overseas Highway. Unobstructed views of the distant horizon are yours in all directions, with the narrow ribbon of highway seemingly suspended between the sky and the sea. Fortunately, turnouts at both ends of the causeway let you take in the vista without worrying about oncoming traffic.

The Long Key Bridge marks the northern end of **Marathon,** a sprawling community that's the second largest in the keys, stretching between MM 65 and MM 47 over a series of islands. One of the visitor highlights of Marathon is at MM 59, on Grassy Key, where the **Dolphin Research Center** (daily; $19.50; 305/289-0002), a rest home for dolphins who've been kept in captivity for too long, is marked by a 30-foot-tall statue of a leaping dolphin. You can swim with a dolphin for around $175.

Accessible by tram from a visitors center in Marathon at MM 48, **Pigeon Key** (daily; $11; 305/743-5999) is one of the least famous but perhaps most fascinating spots along the Overseas Highway. A National Historic District, preserving substantial remnants of the clapboard construction camp that housed some 400 workers employed on the original Seven Mile Bridge from 1912 to 1935, Pigeon Key offers a glimpse of blue-collar Keys history the likes of which you'll find nowhere else.

Lower Keys: Bahia Honda

The old Seven Mile Bridge, which carried first the railroad and later US-1 over Pigeon Key between Marathon and Big Pine Key, was replaced in the early 1980s by a soaring new bridge that gives another batch of breathtaking ocean-to-Gulf views. (The old bridge, which was seen in the Arnold Schwarzenegger/Jamie Lee Curtis movie *True Lies,* still stands below the new one but is now used as a very long fishing pier.)

On Bahia Honda Key, near milemarker 37, you can see a double-decker remnant of the original Keys railroad, with the 1938 **Overseas Highway** supported atop the trestle. Widening the rail bed to accommodate cars was impossible, so a new deck was added to the top of the bridge.

The south end of the Seven Mile Bridge, near MM 40, marks the start of the "Lower Keys," which are considerably less commercial than the others. The best of the Lower Keys is yours to enjoy at MM 36.5, where the entrance to **Bahia Honda State Park** (305/872-2353) leaves the highway behind and brings you back to the way the Keys used to be: covered in palms and coastal hardwood hammocks, with white sand beaches stretching for miles along blue-water seas. Facilities are limited to a few cabins (around $140), a general store, and a snorkel rental stand, but it's a great place to spend some time fishing, beachcombing, sunbathing, or swimming in the deep, warm waters of the Atlantic Ocean or Gulf of Mexico. Camping overnight, the best way to enjoy the sunset, sunrise, and everything in between, costs around $36 a night.

From Bahia Honda, US-1 bends along to Big Pine Key, second largest of the keys and suffering from a bout of suburban mini mall sprawl. Though it looks about as far from natural as can be, Big Pine Key happens to be part of the **National Key Deer Refuge,** set up to protect the increasingly rare Key deer, the "world's smallest deer" at around three feet tall. Some 250 Key deer now live on the island.

The last big key before Key West is Sugarloaf Key, formerly full of pineapple plantations but now known for its **Perky Bat Tower,** a National Historic Landmark alongside US-1 at MM 17. Built by a man named Perky in 1929, the 35-foot tower was designed to house a colony of bats, who were supposed to feast on the plentiful mosquitoes here; however, the bats stayed away, and the mosquitoes stayed put. Sugarloaf Key is also home to the wild **Mangrove Mama's** (305/745-3030), a roadhouse tucked away south of the bridge at MM 20. The seafood and key lime pie is as good as it gets, and there's often live music in the evenings.

Key West

Closer to Cuba than to the U.S. mainland, and still proudly preserving the anarchic spirit of a place that was founded by pirates, **Key West** (pop. 25,478) is definitely a world unto itself. The main drag, Duval Street, has been overrun by tacky souvenir shops, but the rest of Key West is still a great place for aimless wandering.

Just a block from the official "Mile Zero" end of US-1, one of Key West's most popular stops is the **Hemingway House** (daily 9 AM–5 PM; $12), an overgrown mansion on Hwy-A1A at 907 Whitehead Street where the burly writer produced some of his most popular works, including *To Have and Have Not* and *For Whom the Bell Tolls.* Writing in a small cabin connected to the main house by a rope bridge, and spending his nights in the roughneck bar (originally called Sloppy Joe's, now known as Captain

Just so you know, the seashell that's been adopted as a Key West emblem, the **conch,** is pronounced "konk."

Tony's) that still survives at 428 Greene Street, "Papa" Hemingway lived in Key West for about 10 years until his divorce in 1940, when he moved to Havana.

A half mile away, at Whitehead and South Streets, a brightly painted buoy marks the "Southernmost Point in the USA"; next to this is the "Southernmost House." (There's also a "Southernmost Motel.")

At the other end of Duval Street, one place you ought to go—especially if you can time it to be there around sunset— is Mallory Square, which faces west across the Gulf of Mexico and the open Caribbean Sea. Street performers juggle and play music on the broad, brick-paved plaza all day and much of the night. This historic waterfront area is lined by old warehouses and the **Mel Fisher Maritime Museum** (daily; $12), at 200 Greene Street, which displays many millions of dollars worth of jewels, silver, and gold recovered from a pair of 17th-century Spanish shipwrecks.

Key West Practicalities

Amid the tourist clutter, Key West holds a range of fabulous restaurants, enough to suit all tastes and budgets. Capturing the eccentric Key West spirit for over 20 years, kid-friendly **Camille's** (305/296-4811), at 1202 Simonton Street, serves crisp waffles, sandwiches, and delicious dinners every day. For a memorable dinner, **Antonia's** (305/294-6565) at 615 Duval has truly excellent Italian food: great fresh pastas, perfect lasagnas, and awesome grilled meats. But for a real taste of Key West, you can't beat **B.O.'s Fishwagon** (305/294-9272), a ramshackle fish stand a block from the water and three blocks north of Duval at 801 Caroline Street—soft-shell crab and oyster po' boys, fresh mahi fish-and-chips, cold beer, and frequent live blues bands make this a great place to soak up Key West's party-hardy-at-the-end-of-the-world ambience.

The aforementioned **Southernmost Motel in the USA** ($95 and up; 305/296-6577), at 1319 Duval Street, has a poolside bar and AAA-rated rooms. A surprisingly desirable option is the **Crowne Plaza** ($150 and up; 305/296-2991) at 430 Duval Street, which plasters its chain-hotel name on the facade of the La Concha Hotel, one of Key West's oldest and largest hotels, but otherwise preserves the historic 1920s character; you can't get more central than this. There are also many nice old B&Bs around Key West, like the landmark **Old Town Manor** ($150 and up; 305/292-2170), at 511 Eaton Street, an 1880s Greek Revival mansion with a gorgeous garden.

The official end of US-1 is marked by a zero milepost sign in front of the Key West post office, on Truman Avenue.

Key West is the end of the Overseas Highway, but it's not the end of the sightseeing opportunities, so if you don't want to turn around and head home just yet, you don't have to. You can board a sunset cruise, or take a seaplane tour of historic **Fort Jefferson,** a photogenic 150-year-old fortress and prison located on an island in **Dry Tortugas National Park,** 68 miles west of Key West. Prisoners held here included the hapless doctor Samuel Mudd, who set the broken leg of Lincoln assassin John Wilkes Booth.

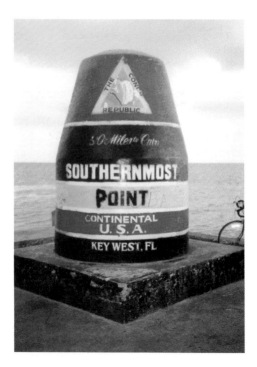

Index

Photo and Illustration Credits

United States Quarter-Dollar Coin Images

United States Postage Stamps

Additional Credits:

Cover Images: